Hezekiah Butterworth

The Log School-House on the Columbia

A Tale of the Pioneers of the Great Northwest

Hezekiah Butterworth

The Log School-House on the Columbia
A Tale of the Pioneers of the Great Northwest

ISBN/EAN: 9783744666435

Printed in Europe, USA, Canada, Australia, Japan

Cover: Foto ©ninafisch / pixelio.de

More available books at **www.hansebooks.com**

THE LOG SCHOOL-HOUSE ON THE COLUMBIA

A TALE OF THE PIONEERS OF THE GREAT NORTHWEST

BY

HEZEKIAH BUTTERWORTH
AUTHOR OF THE ZIGZAG BOOKS

ILLUSTRATED

NEW YORK
D. APPLETON AND COMPANY
1890

COPYRIGHT, 1890,
BY D. APPLETON AND COMPANY.

PREFACE.

A YEAR or more ago one of the librarians in charge of the young people's books in the Boston Public Library called my attention to the fact that there were few books of popular information in regard to the pioneers of the great Northwest. The librarian suggested that I should write a story that would give a view of the heroic lives of the pioneers of Oregon and Washington.

Soon after this interview I met a distinguished educator who had lately returned from the Columbia River, who told me the legend of the old chief who died of grief in the grave of his son, somewhat in the manner described in this volume. The legend had those incidental qualities that haunt a susceptible imagination, and it was told to me in such a dramatic way that I could not put it out of my mind.

A few weeks after hearing this haunting legend

I went over the Rocky Mountains by the Canadian Pacific Railway, and visited the Columbia River and the scenes associated with the Indian story. I met in Washington, Yesler, Denney, and Hon. Elwood Evans, the historian; visited the daughter of Seattle, the chief, "Old Angeline"; and gathered original stories in regard to the pioneers of the Puget Sound country from many sources. In this atmosphere the legend grew upon me, and the outgrowth of it is this volume, which, amid a busy life of editorial and other work, has forced itself upon my experience.

H. B.

28 WORCESTER STREET, BOSTON, *July 4, 1890.*

CONTENTS.

CHAPTER	PAGE
I.—Gretchen's Violin	9
II.—The Chief of the Cascades	27
III.—"Boston Tilicum"	43
IV.—Mrs. Woods's Tame Bear, Little "Roll Over"	67
V.—The Nest of the Fishing Eagle	75
VI.—The Mountain Lion	86
VII.—The "Smoke-Talk"	95
VIII.—The Black Eagle's Nest of the Falls of the Missouri	114
IX.—Gretchen's Visit to the Old Chief of the Cascades	127
X.—Mrs. Woods meets Little "Roll Over" again	146
XI.—Marlowe Mann's New Robinson Crusoe	154
XII.—Old Joe Meek and Mr. Spaulding	162
XIII.—A Warning	170
XIV.—The Potlatch	181
XV.—The Traumerei again	196

CONTENTS.

CHAPTER	PAGE
XVI.—A SILENT TRIBE	204
XVII.—A DESOLATE HOME AND A DESOLATE PEOPLE	215
XVIII.—THE LIFTED CLOUD—THE INDIANS COME TO THE SCHOOLMASTER	221

HISTORICAL NOTES.

I. Vancouver	229
II. The Oregon Trail	232
III. Governor Stevens	236
IV. Seattle the Chief	239
V. Whitman's Ride for Oregon	244
VI. Mount Saint Helens	250

LIST OF ILLUSTRATIONS.

		PAGE
Gretchen at the Potlatch Feast .	. *E. J. Austen*	
	Frontispiece	
Indians spearing fish at Salmon Falls		16
"Here were mountains grander than Olympus." The North Puyallup Glacier, Mount Tacoma . .		28
In the midst of this interview Mrs. Woods appeared at the door of the cabin	. *A. E. Pope* . .	72
The eagle soared away in the blue heavens, and the flag streamed after him in his talons . .	. *E. J. Austen* .	84
The mountain lion . . .	. *D. Carter Beard* .	92
An Indian village on the Columbia .		130
Afar loomed Mount Hood . . .		135
A castellated crag arose solitary and solemn		142
At the Cascades of the Columbia .		183
Multnomah Falls in earlier years.		
	Redrawn by Walter C. Greenough	205
The old chief stood stoical and silent .	*E. J. Austen* .	209
Middle block-house at the Cascades .		242

THE LOG SCHOOL-HOUSE ON THE COLUMBIA.

CHAPTER I.

GRETCHEN'S VIOLIN.

An elderly woman and a German girl were walking along the old Indian trail that led from the northern mountains to the Columbia River. The river was at this time commonly called the Oregon, as in Bryant's poem:

> "Where rolls the Oregon,
> And no sound is heard save its own dashings."

The girl had a light figure, a fair, open face, and a high forehead with width in the region of ideality, and she carried under her arm a long black case in which was a violin. The woman had lived in one of the valleys of the Oregon for several years, but the German girl had recently arrived in one of the colonies that had lately come to the territory under the missionary agency of the Rev. Jason Lee.

There came a break in the tall, cool pines that lined the trail and that covered the path with glimmering shadows. Through the opening the high summits of Mount St. Helens glittered like a city of pearl, far, far away in the clear, bright air. The girl's blue eyes opened wide, and her feet stumbled.

"There, there you go again down in the hollow! Haven't you any eyes? I would think you had by the looks of them. Well, Gretchen, they were placed right in the front of your head so as to look forward; they would have been put in the top of your head if it had been meant that you should look up to the sky in that way. What is it you see?"

"Oh, mother, I wish I was—an author."

"An author! What put that into your simple head? You meant to say you would like to be a poet, but you didn't dare to, because you know I don't approve of such things. People who get such flighty ideas into their loose minds always find the world full of hollows. No, Gretchen, I am willing you should play on the violin, though some of the Methody do not approve of that; and that you should finger the musical glasses in the evening

—they have a religious sound and soothe me, like; but the reading of poetry and novels I never did countenance, except Methody hymns and the 'Fool of Quality,' and as for the writing of poetry, it is a Boston notion and an ornary habit. Nature is all full of poetry out here, and what this country needs is pioneers, not poets."

There came into view another opening among the pines as the two went on. The sun was ascending a cloudless sky, and far away in the cerulean arch of glimmering splendors the crystal peaks and domes of St. Helens appeared again.

The girl stopped.

"What now?" said the woman, testily.

"Look—yonder!"

"Look yonder—what for? That's nothing but a mountain, a great waste of land all piled up to the sky, and covered with a lot of ice and snow. I don't see what they were made for, any way—just to make people go round, I suppose, so that the world will not be too easy for them."

"Oh, mother, I do not see how you can feel so out here! I never dreamed of anything so beautiful!"

"Feel so out here! What do you mean? Haven't I always been good to you? Didn't I give you a good home in Lynn after your father and mother died? Wasn't I a mother to you? Didn't I nurse you through the fever? Didn't I send for you to come way out here with the immigrants, and did you ever find a better friend in the world than I have been to you?"

"Yes, mother, but—"

"And don't I let you play the violin, which the Methody elder didn't much approve of?"

"Yes, mother, you have always been good to me, and I love you more than anybody else on earth."

There swept into view a wild valley of giant trees, and rose clear above it, a scene of overwhelming magnificence.

"Oh, mother, I can hardly look at it—isn't it splendid? It makes me feel like crying."

The practical, resolute woman was about to say, "Well, look the other way then," but she checked the rude words. The girl had told her that she loved her more than any one else in the world, and the confession had touched her heart.

"Well, Gretchen, that mountain used to make me feel so sometimes when I first came out here. I always thought that the mountains would look *peakeder* than they do. I didn't think that they would take up so much of the land. I suppose that they are all well enough in their way, but a pioneer woman has no time for sentiments, except hymns. I don't feel like you now, and I don't think that I ever did. I couldn't learn to play the violin and the musical glasses if I were to try, and I am sure that I should never go out into the woodshed to try to rhyme *sun* with *fun;* no, Gretchen, all such follies as these I should *shun*. What difference does it make whether a word rhymes with one word or another?"

To the eye of the poetic and musical German girl the dead volcano, with its green base and frozen rivers and dark, glimmering lines of carbon, seemed like a fairy tale, a celestial vision, an ascent to some city of crystal and pearl in the sky. To her foster mother the stupendous scene was merely a worthless waste, as to Wordsworth's unspiritual wanderer:

> "A primrose by the river's brim,
> A yellow primrose was to him,
> And it was nothing more."

She was secretly pleased at Gretchen's wonder and surprise at the new country, but somehow she felt it her duty to talk querulously, and to check the flow of the girl's emotions, which she did much to excite. Her own life had been so circumscribed and hard that the day seemed to be too bright to be speaking the truth. She peered into the sky for a cloud, but there was none, on this dazzling Oregon morning. The trail now opened for a long way before the eyes of the travelers. Far ahead gleamed the pellucid waters of the Columbia, or Oregon. Half-way between them and the broad, rolling river a dark, tall figure appeared.

"Gretchen?"

"What, mother?"

"Gretchen, look! There goes the Yankee schoolmaster. Came way out here over the mountains to teach the people of the wilderness, and all for nothing, too. That shows that people have souls —some people have. Walk right along beside me, proper-like. You needn't ever tell any one that I ain't your true mother. If I ain't ashamed of you, you needn't be ashamed of me. I wish that you were my own girl, now that you have said that you love me more than anybody else in the world. That remark kind o' touched me. I know that I sometimes talk hard, but I mean well, and I have to tell you the plain truth so as to do my duty by you, and then I won't have anything to reflect upon.

"Just look at him! Straight as an arrow!

They say that his folks are rich. Come out here way over the mountains, and is just going to teach school in a log school-house—all made of logs and sods and mud-plaster, adobe they call it—a graduate of Harvard College, too."

A long, dark object appeared in the trees covered with bark and moss. Behind these trees was a waterfall, over which hung the crowns of pines. The sunlight sifted through the odorous canopy, and fell upon the strange, dark object that lay across the branching limbs of two ancient trees.

Gretchen stopped again.

" Mother, what is that ? "

" A grave—an Indian grave."

The Indians bury their dead in the trees out here, or used to do so. A brown hawk arose from the mossy coffin and winged its way wildly into the sunny heights of the air. It had made its nest on the covering of the body. These new scenes were all very strange to the young German girl.

The trail was bordered with young ferns; wild violets lay in beds of purple along the running streams, and the mountain phlox with its kindling buds carpeted the shelving ways under the murmuring pines. The woman and girl came at last to a wild, open space; before them rolled the Oregon, beyond it stretched a great treeless plain, and over it towered a gigantic mountain,* in whose crown, like a jewel, shone a resplendent glacier.

Just before them, on the bluffs of the river, under three gigantic evergreens, each of which was more than two hundred feet high, stood an odd structure of logs and sods, which the builders called the Sod School-house. It was not a sod school-house in the sense in which the term has been applied to more recent structures in the treeless prairie districts of certain mid-ocean States; it was rudely framed of pine, and was furnished with a pine desk and benches.

Along the river lay a plateau full of flowers, birds, and butterflies, and over the great river and flowering plain the clear air glimmered. Like some sun-god's abode in the shadow of ages, St. Helens still lifted her silver tents in the far sky. Eagles and mountain birds wheeled, shrieking joyously, here and there. Below the bluffs the silent salmon-fishers awaited their prey, and down the river with paddles apeak drifted the bark canoes of Cayuses and Umatillas.

A group of children were gathered about the open door of the new school-house, and among them

Indians spearing fish at Salmon Falls.

rose the tall form of Marlowe Mann, the Yankee schoolmaster.

He had come over the mountains some years before in the early expeditions organized and directed by Dr. Marcus Whitman, of the American Board of Missions. Whether the mission to the Cayuses and Walla Wallas, which Dr. Whitman established on the bend of the Columbia, was then regarded as a home or foreign field of work, we can not say. The doctor's solitary ride of four thousand miles, in order to save the great Northwest territory to the United States, is one of the most poetic and dramatic episodes of American history. It has proved to be worth to our country more than all the money that has been given to missionary enterprises. Should the Puget Sound cities become the great ports of Asia, and the ships of commerce drift from Seattle and Tacoma over the Japan current to the Flowery Isles and China; should the lumber, coal, minerals, and wheat-fields of Washington, Oregon, Montana, and Idaho at last compel these cities to rival New York and Boston, the populous empire will owe to the patriotic missionary zeal of Dr. Whitman a debt which it can only pay in honor and love. Dr. Whitman was murdered by the Indians soon after the settlement of the Walla Walla country by the pioneers from the Eastern States.

Mr. Mann's inspiration to become a missionary pioneer on the Oregon had been derived from a Boston schoolmaster whose name also the Northwest should honor. An inspired soul with a prophet's vision usually goes before the great movements of life; solitary men summon the march of progress, then decrease while others increase. Hall J. Kelley was a teacher of the olden time, well known in Boston almost a century ago. He became possessed with the idea that Oregon was destined to become a great empire. He collected all possible information about the territory, and organized emigration schemes, the first of which started from St. Louis in 1828, and failed. He talked of Oregon continually. The subject haunted him day and night. It was he who inspired Rev. Jason Lee, the pioneer of the Willamette Valley. Lee interested Senator Linn, of Missouri, in Oregon, and this senator, on December 11, 1838, introduced the bill into Congress which organized the Territory.

Some of the richly endowed new schools of Oregon would honor history by a monumental recognition of the name of Hall J. Kelley, the old schoolmaster, whose dreams were of the Columbia, and who inspired some of his pupils to become resolute pioneers. Boston was always a friend to Washington and Oregon. Where the old schoolmaster now rests we do not know. Probably in a neglected grave amid the briers and mosses of some old cemetery on the Atlantic coast.

When Marlowe Mann came to the Northwest he found the Indian tribes unquiet and suspicious of the new settlements. One of the pioneers had caused a sickness among some thievish Indians by putting emetic poison in watermelons. The Indians believed these melons to have been conjured by the white doctor, and when other sickness came among them, they attributed it to the same cause. The massacre at Waülaptu and the murder of Whitman grew in part out of these events.

Mr. Mann settled near the old Chief of the Cascades. He sought the Indian friendship of this chief, and asked him for his protection.

"People fulfill the expectation of the trust put in them—Indians as well as children," he used to say. "A boy fulfills the ideals of his mother—what the mother believes the boy will be, that he will become. Treat a thief as though he were honest, and he will be honest with you. We help people to be better by believing in what is good in them. I am going to trust the friendship of the old Chief of the Cascades, and he will never betray it."

It was summer, and there was to be a great Indian Potlatch feast under the autumn moon. The Potlatch is a feast of gifts. It is usually a peaceful gathering of friendly tribes, with rude music and gay dances; but it bodes war and massacre and danger if it end with the dance of the evil spirits, or the devil dance, as it has been known—a dance which the English Government has recently forbidden among the Northwestern tribes.

The Indians were demanding that the great fall Potlatch should end with this ominous dance of fire and besmearings of blood. The white people everywhere were disturbed by these reports, for they feared what might be the secret intent of this wild revel. The settlers all regarded with apprehension the October moon.

The tall schoolmaster watched the approach of Mrs. Woods and Gretchen with a curious interest. The coming of a pupil with no books and a violin was something unexpected. He stepped forward with a courtly grace and greeted them most politely, for wherever Marlowe Mann might be, he never forgot that he was a gentleman.

"This is my gal what I have brought to be educated," said Mrs. Woods, proudly. "They think a great deal of education up around Boston where I came from. Where did you come from?"

"From Boston."

"So I have been told—from Harvard College. Can I speak with you a minute in private?"

"Yes, madam. Step aside."

"I suppose you are kinder surprised that I let my gal there, Gretchen, bring her violin with her; but I have a secret to tell ye. Gretchen is a kind of a poet, makes rhymes, she does; makes *fool* rhyme with *school*, and such things as that. Now, I don't take any interest in such things. But she does play the violin beautiful. Learned of a German teacher. Now, do you want to know why I let her bring her violin? Well, I thought it might *help* you. You've got a hard lot of scholars to deal with out here, and there are Injuns around, too, and one never knows what they may do.

"Well, schoolmaster, you never heard nothin' like that violin. It isn't no evil spirit that is in Gretchen's violin; it's an angel. I first noticed it one day when husband and I had been havin' some words. We have words sometimes. I have a lively mind, and know how to use words when I am opposed. Well, one day when husband and I had been havin' words, which we shouldn't, seein' we are Methody, Gretchen began to cry, and went and got her violin, and began to play just like a bird. And my high temper all melted away, and my mind went back to the old farm in New England, and I declare, schoolmaster, I just threw my apron over my head and began to cry, and I told Gretchen never to play that tune again when I was talking to husband for his good.

"Well, one day there came a lot of Injuns to the house and demanded fire-water. I am Methody, and don't keep any such things in the house. Husband is a sober, honest man. Now, I've always noticed that an Injun is a coward, and I think the best way to get along with Injuns is to appear not to fear them. So I ordered the stragglers away, when one of them swung his tommyhawk about my head, and the others threatened to kill me. How my heart did beat! Gretchen began to cry; then she ran all at once for her violin and played the very same tune, and the Injuns just stood like so many dumb statues and listened, and, when the tune was over, one of them said 'Spirits,' and they all went away like so many children.

"Now, I thought you would like to hear my gal play between schools, and, if ever you should get into any trouble with your scholars or Injuns or anybody, just call upon Gretchen, and she will play that tune on the violin."

"What wonderful tune is it, madam?"

"I don't know. I don't know one tune from another, though I do sing the old Methody hymns that I learned in Lynn when I am about my work. I don't know whether she knows or not. She learned it of a German."

"I am glad that you let her bring the instrument. I once played the violin myself in the orchestra of the Boston Handel and Haydn Society."

"Did you? Then you like it. I have a word or two more to say about Gretchen. She's a good gal, and shows her bringing up. Teach her reading, writing, and figures. You needn't teach her no grammar. I could always talk without any grammar, in the natural way. I was a bound-girl, and never had much education. I have had my ups and downs in life, like all the rest of the world. You will do the best you can for Gretchen, won't you?"

"Yes, my dear madam, and for every one. I

try to make every one true to the best that is in them. I am glad to have Gretchen for a scholar. I will speak to her by and by."

How strange was the scene to Gretchen! She remembered the winding Rhine, with its green hills and terraced vineyards and broken-walled castles; Basel and the singing of the student clubs in the gardens on summer evenings; the mountain-like church at Strasburg; and the old streets of Mayence. She recalled the legends and music of the river of song—a river that she had once thought to be the most beautiful on earth. But what were the hills of the Rhine to the scenery that pierced the blue sky around her, and how light seemed the river itself to the majestic flow of the Columbia! Yet the home-land haunted her. Would she go back again? How would her real parents have felt had they known that she would have found a home here in the wilderness? Why had Providence led her steps here? Her mother had been a pious Lutheran. Had she been led here to help in some future mission to the Indian race?

"Dreaming?" said Mrs. Woods. "Well, I suppose it can't be helped. If a body has the misfortune to be kiting off to the clouds, going up like an eagle and coming down like a goose, it can't be helped. There are a great many things that can't be helped in this world, and all we can do is to make the best of them. Some people were born to live in the skies, and it makes it hard for those who have to try to live with them. Job suffered some things, but—I won't scold out here—I have my trials; but it may be they are all for the best, as the Scripture says."

These forbearing remarks were not wholly meant for Gretchen's reproval. Mrs. Woods liked to have the world know that she had her trials, and she was pleased to find so many ears on this bright morning open to her experiences.

She liked to say to Gretchen things that were meant for other ears; there was novelty in the indirection. She also was accustomed to quote freely from the Scriptures and from the Methodist hymn-book, which was almost her only accomplishment. She had led a simple, hard-working life in her girlhood; had become a follower of Jason Lee during one of the old-time revivals of religion; had heard of the Methodist emigration to Oregon, and wished to follow it. She hardly knew why. Though rough in speech and somewhat peculiar, she was a kind-hearted and an honest woman, and very industrious and resolute. Mr. Lee saw in her the spirit of a pioneer, and advised her to join his colony. She married Mr. Woods, went to the Dalles of the Columbia, and afterward to her present home upon a donation claim.

CHAPTER II.

THE CHIEF OF THE CASCADES.

MARLOWE MANN was a graduate of Harvard in the classic period of the college. He had many scholarly gifts, and as many noble qualities of soul as mental endowments. He was used to the oratory of Henry Ware and young Edward Everett, and had known Charles Sumner and Wendell Phillips at college, when the Greek mind and models led the young student in his fine development, and made him a Pericles in his dreams.

But the young student of this heroic training, no matter how well conditioned his family, usually turned from his graduation to some especial mission in life. "I must put myself into a cause," said young Wendell Phillips. Charles Sumner espoused the struggle of the negro for freedom, and said: "To this cause do I offer all I have." Marlowe Mann was a member of the historic Old South Church, like Phillips in his early years. There was an enthusiasm for missions in the churches of Boston then, and he began to dream of Oregon and the mysterious empire of the great Northwest, as pictured by the old schoolmaster, Kelley; just at this time came Dr. Whitman to the East, half frozen from his long ride, and asked to lead an emigration to Walla Walla, to save the Northern empire to the territory of the States. He heard the doctor's thrilling story of how he had unfurled the flag over the open Bible on the crags that looked down on the valleys of the Oregon, and his resolution was made. He did not follow Dr. Whitman on the first expedition of colonists, but joined him a year or two afterward. He built him a log-cabin on the Columbia, and gave his whole soul to teaching, missionary work among the Indians, and to bringing emigrants from the East.

The country thrilled him—its magnificent scenery, the grandeur of the Columbia, the vastness of the territory, and the fertility of the soil. Here were mountains grander than Olympus, and harbors and water-courses as wonderful as the Ægean. He was almost afraid to map the truth in his extensive correspondence with the East, lest it should seem so incredible as to defeat his purpose.

When the log school-house was building, Mr.

The North Puyallup Glacier, Mount Tacoma.

Mann had gone to the old Chief of the Cascades and had invited him to send his Indian boy to the school. He had shown him what an advantage it would be to the young chief to understand more thoroughly Chinook and English. He was wise and politic in the matter as well as large-hearted, for he felt that the school might need the friendliness of the old chief, and in no way could it be better secured.

"The world treats you as you treat the world," he said; "and what you are to the world, the world is to you. Tell me only what kind of a neighborhood you come from, and I will tell you what kind of a neighborhood you are going to; we all see the world in ourselves. I will educate the boy, and his father will protect the school. The Indian heart is hot and revengeful, but it is honest and true. I intend to be honest with the Indians in all things, and if there should occur a dance of the evil spirits at the Potlatch, no harm will ever come to the log school-house; and I do not believe that such a dance with evil intent to the settlers will ever take place. Human nature is all one book everywhere."

As he stood there that morning, with uncovered head, an unexpected event happened. The children suddenly said:

"Look!" and "Umatilla!"

Out of the forest came an aged Indian, of gigantic stature—Umatilla, one of the chiefs of the Cascades; and beside him walked his only son, the Light of the Eagle's Plume, or, as he had been named by the English, Benjamin.

Umatilla, like Massasoit, of the early colonial history of Plymouth, was a remarkable person. Surrounded by warlike tribes, he had been a man of peace. He was a lover of Nature, and every shining cloud to his eye was a chariot. He personified everything, like the ancient Greeks. He talked in poetic figures; to him the sky was alive, every event had a soul, and his mind had dwelt upon the great truths of Nature until he had become more of a philosopher than a ruler.

He had been the father of a large family, but six of his sons had died of the plague, or rather of the treatment which the medicine-men had used in the disease, which was to sweat the victims in hot earthen ovens, and then plunge them into the Columbia.

His whole heart in his old age was fixed upon his only son, Benjamin. The two were seldom separated. To make the boy happy was the end of the old chief's life.

The two approached the courtly schoolmaster.

"White master," said the old chief, "I have brought to you the Light of the Eagle's Plume. He is my heart, and will be the heart of my people when my suns are all passed over and my stars gone out. Will you teach him to be a good chief? I want him to know English, and how to worship the Master of Life. Will you take him to your school lodge?"

The tall master bowed low, and took the Indian boy by the hand.

The boy was a princely youth. His figure would have held the eye of a sculptor in long admiration. The chisel of a Phidias could hardly have exceeded such a form. His features were like the Roman, his eye quick and lustrous, and his lips noble and kindly. He wore a blanket over his shoulders, gathered in a long sash, ornamented with shells, about his loins, and a crest of eagle plumes and shells on his head indicated his rank and dignity. He could speak some words of Chinook, and English imperfectly. He had mingled much with the officers of the Hudson Bay Company, and so had learned many of the customs of civilization.

"I am honored," said the courtly, tall schoolmaster, "in having such a youth for my pupil. Chief of the Umatillas, I thank thee. All that is good in me will I give to your noble boy. I live with my eye upon the future; the work of my life is to lead people to follow their better natures and to be true to their best selves. There is a good angel in all men here"—he put his hand on his heart—"it leads men away from evil; it seeks the way of life; its end is yonder with the Infinite. Chief of the Umatillas, I will try to teach the young man to follow it. Do you understand?"

The aged chief bowed. He caught the meaning of the thought, if not of the rather formal words. He comprehended the idea that the tall schoolmaster believed goodness to be immortal. The regions of the Cascades were indeed beautiful with their ancient forests and gleaming mountain walls, but he had been taught to believe that the great Master of Life had provided eternal scenes that transcended these for those who were worthy to receive them.

An unexpected turn came to this stately and pacific interview. Mrs. Woods was piqued at the deference that the tall schoolmaster had shown to the chief and his son. She walked about restlessly, cut a rod from one of the trees with a large knife which she always carried with her, and at last called the master aside again.

"Say, mister, here. You ain't going to take that young Injun into your school, are you? There'll be trouble, now, if you do. Know Injuns —you don't. You are young, but 'tain't best for you to eat all your apples green. I've always been very particular about the company I keep, if I was born poor and have had to work hard, and never studied no foreign languages. I warn you!"

She raised her voice, and Benjamin heard what she had said. He suspected her ill-will toward him from her manner, but he comprehended the meaning of her last words.

He at first looked puzzled and grieved, then suddenly his thin lips were pressed together; the passion of anger was possessing him, soon to be followed by the purpose of revenge.

Mrs. Woods saw that she had gone too far in the matter, and that her spirit and meaning had been discovered by the son of the chief. The danger to which she had exposed herself made her nervous. But she began to act on her old principle never to show fear in the presence of an Indian.

"Here, mister, I must go now," she said, in a loud voice. "Take this rod, and govern your school like a man. If I were a teacher, I'd make my scholars smart in more ways than one." She held out the rod to the master.

There was a movement in the air like a flash. Benjamin, with noiseless feet, had slipped up behind her. He had conceived the idea that the offer of the rod somehow meant enmity to him. He seized the rod from behind the woman, and, sweeping it through the air, with kindled eye and glowing cheeks, wheeled before the master.

"Boston tilicum, don't you dare!"

"Boston tilicum" was the Chinook for an American, and the Chinook or trade language had become common to all the tribes on the Columbia. The early American traders on the Northern Pacific coast were from Boston.

He raised the rod aloft defiantly like a young champion, and presented a heroic figure, which excited the tremulous admiration and wonder of the little group. He then pointed it toward Mrs. Woods, and said contemptuously in Chinook:

"Cloochman!" (woman).

The scene changed to the comical. Mrs. Woods snatched off her broad sun-bonnet, revealing her gray hair, and assumed an appearance of defiance, though her heart was really trembling with fear.

"I ain't afraid of no Injuns," she said, "and I don't take any impudence from anybody. I've had to fight the whole world all my life, and I've always conquered. There—now—there!"

She whipped the rod out of the young Indian's hand.

Benjamin's eyes blazed.

"Closche nanitch" (look out), he said. "I am an Umatilla. Siwash (Indian) will remember. There are hawks in the sky."

"Kamooks" (dog), returned Mrs. Woods, defiantly. "Kamooks."

She would have said "cultus" had she dared. "Cultus" is the most insulting word that can be applied to an Indian, and, when it is used, it invites the most deadly revenge. The word had come to her lips, but she had not the courage to invoke the consequences of such a taunt.

But the young Indian further excited her. He shook the rod at her, and her passion mastered her prudence. She struggled with herself, and was silent for a few moments. But, suddenly catching the young Indian's eye, which had in it a savage triumph, she exclaimed:

"Cultus Umatilla—"

The old chief stepped forward and lifted his hands.

"Pil-pil" (blood), said Benjamin. "There are hawks in the air—"

"Be still!" said the chief.

"—they whet their beaks," continued Benjamin. "Potlatch!"

The whole company were filled with excitement or terror. Gretchen trembled, and began to cry. Three Indians were seen coming down the trail, and the sight seemed to fill Benjamin with a mysterious delight. Mrs. Woods saw them with secret fear, and the master with apprehension. Several of the children began to cry, and there was a look of pain, terror, or distress on all the faces.

Suddenly Gretchen stepped apart from the group and lifted to her shoulder her violin.

A hunting strain rose on the bright morning air. It seemed like the flight of a singing bird.

The chief's arms dropped. The music arose like a sweet memory of all that is good and beautiful.

The three Indians stopped to listen. The music became more sweet and entrancing. The anger went out of Benjamin's face, and there came better feelings into his soul.

The music breathed of the Rhine, of vineyards and festivals, but he understood it not; to him it recalled the mysterious legends of the Umatillas, the mysteries of life, and the glory of the heroes who slept on the island of the dead or amid the sweetly sighing branches of the trees. The air was the *Traumerei*.

When the music ceased there was a long silence. In it Mrs. Woods turned away slowly, with a word of advice to Gretchen that under other circumstances would have appeared amusing:

"Behave yourself like a lady," she said, "and remember your bringing up. Good-morning to ye all."

The little group watched her as she moved safely away. A little black bear crossed her path as she was entering the wood, and stopped on the way. But her steps were growing rapid, and, as she did not seem to regard him as a matter of any consequence, he turned and ran. The company smiled, and so the peril of the morning seemed to pass away.

The scene would have been comical but for the painful look in the kindly face of the old Chief of the Cascades. He had come toward the schoolhouse with high hopes, and what had happened caused him pain. The word "Potlatch," spoken by the Indian boy, had caused his brow to cloud and his face to turn dark.

"We will all go into the house," said the master. "Umatilla, will you not honor us with a visit this morning?"

"No—me come this afternoon for the boy; me wait for him outside. Boston tilicum, let me speak to you a little. I am a father."

"Yes, and a good father."

"I am a father—you no understand—Boston tilicum—father. I want you to teach him like a father—not you understand?"

"Yes, I understand."

"Father—teacher—you, Boston tilicum."

"Yes, I understand, and I will be a father teacher to your Benjamin."

"I die some day. You understand?"

"Yes, I understand."

"You understand, Boston tilicum, you understand. What I want my boy to become that I am for my boy. That you be."

"Yes, Umatilla, I believe an Indian's word—you may trust mine. I will be to your boy what you may have him become. The Indian is true to his friends. I believe in *you*. I will be true."

The old chief drew his blanket round him proudly.

"Boston tilicum," said he, "if ever the day of trouble comes, I will protect you and the log school-house. You may trust my word. Indian speak true."

The tall schoolmaster bowed.

"Nika atte cepa" (I like you much), said the chief. "Potlatch shall no harm you. Klahyam klahhye—am!" (Good-by).

Mrs. Woods hurried homeward and tried to calm her excited mind by singing a very heroic old hymn:

> "Come on, my partners in distress,
> My comrades in the wilderness,
> Who still your bodies feel."

The blue skies gleamed before her, and overhead wheeled a golden eagle. To her it was an emblem, a good omen, and her spirit became quiet and happy amid all the contradictions of her rough life. She sat down at last on the log before her door, with the somewhat strange remark:

"I do hate Injuns; *nevertheless*—"

Mrs. Woods was accustomed to correct the wrong tendencies of her heart and tongue by this word "nevertheless," which she used as an incomplete sentence. This "nevertheless" seemed to express her better self; to correct the rude tendencies of her nature. Had she been educated in her early days, this tendency to self-correction would have made her an ideal woman, but she owed nearly all her intellectual training to the sermons of the Rev. Jason Lee, which she had heard in some obscure corner of a room, or in Methodist chapel, or under the trees.

Her early experience with the Indians had not made her a friend to the native races, notwithstanding the missionary labors of the Rev. Jason Lee. The first Indian that made her a visit on the donation claim did not leave a favorable impression on her mind.

This Indian had come to her door while she was engaged in the very hard work of sawing wood. He had never seen a saw before, and, as it seemed to him to be a part of the woman herself, he approached her with awe and wonder. That the saw should eat through the wood appeared to him a veritable miracle.

Mrs. Woods, unaware of her visitor, paused to take breath, looked up, beheld the tall form with staring eyes, and started back.

"Medicine-woman—conjure!" said the Indian, in Chinook.

Mrs. Woods was filled with terror, but a moment's thought recalled her resolution. She lifted her hand, and, pointing to the saw in the wood, she said, with a commanding tone:

"Saw!"

The Indian obeyed awkwardly, and wondering at the progress of the teeth of the saw through the wood. It was a hot day; the poor Indian soon became tired, and stopped work with a beating heart and bursting veins.

"Saw—saw!" said Mrs. Woods, with a sweep of her hands, as though some mysterious fate depended upon the order.

The saw went very hard now, for he did not know how to use it, and the wood was hard, and the Indian's only thought seemed to be how to escape. Mrs. Woods held him in her power by a kind of mental magnetism, like that which Queen Margaret exercised over the robber.

"Water!" at last gasped the Indian.

"Saw—saw!" said Mrs. Woods; then turned away to bring him water.

When she looked around again, an unexpected sight met her eyes. The Indian was flying away, taking the saw with him. She never beheld either again, and it was a long time before any Indian appeared at the clearing after this odd event, though Mrs. Woods ultimately had many adventures among the wandering Siwashes.

A saw was no common loss in these times of but few mechanical implements in Oregon, and Mrs. Woods did not soon forgive the Indian for taking away what he probably regarded as an instrument of torture.

"I do hate Injuns!" she would often say; but quite likely would soon after be heard singing one of the hymns of the missionaries at the Dalles:

> "O'er Columbia's wide-spread forests
> Haste, ye heralds of the Lamb;
> Teach the red man, wildly roaming,
> Faith in Immanuel's name,"

which, if poor poetry, was very inspiring.

CHAPTER III.

BOSTON TILICUM.

MARLOWE MANN—"Boston tilicum," as the Siwashes called all the missionaries, teachers, and traders from the East—sat down upon a bench of split log and leaned upon his desk, which consisted of two split logs in a rough frame. A curious school confronted him. His pupils numbered fifteen, representing Germany, England, Sweden, New England, and the Indian race.

"The world will some day come to the Yankee schoolmaster," he used to say to the bowery halls of old Cambridge; and this prophecy, which had come to him on the banks of the Charles, seemed indeed to be beginning to be fulfilled on the Columbia.

He opened the school in the same serene and scholarly manner as he would have done in a school in Cambridge.

"He is not a true gentleman who is not one

under all conditions and circumstances," was one of his views of a well-clothed character; and this morning he addressed the school with the courtesy of an old college professor.

"I have come here," he said, "with but one purpose, and that is to try to teach you things which will do you the most good in life. That is always the best which will do the most good; all else is inferior. I shall first teach you to obey your sense of right in all things. This is the first principle of a true education. You will always know the way of life if you have this principle for your guide.

"Conscience is the first education. A man's spiritual nature is his highest nature, and his spiritual concerns transcend all others. If a man is spiritually right, he is the master of all things. I would impress these truths on your minds, and teach them at the beginning. I have become willing to be poor, and to walk life's ways alone. The pilot of the Argo never returned from Colchis, but the Argo itself returned with the Golden Fleece. It may be so with my work; if so, I will be content. I have selected for our Scripture lesson the 'incorruptible seed.'"

He rose and spoke like one before an august

assembly; and so it was to him, with his views of the future of the great empire of the Northwest. A part of the pupils could not comprehend all that he said any more than they had understood the allusion to the pilot of the Argo; but his manner was so gracious, so earnest, so inspired, that they all felt the spirit of it, and some had come to regard themselves as the students of some great destiny.

"Older domes than the pyramids are looking down upon you," he said, "and you are born to a higher destiny than were ever the children of the Pharaohs."

With the exception of Gretchen, not one of the pupils fully understood the picturesque allusion. Like the reference to the pilot of the Argo, it was poetic mystery to them; and yet it filled them with a noble curiosity to know much and a desire to study hard, and to live hopefully and worthily. Like the outline of some unknown mountain range, it allured them to higher outlooks and wider distances.

"He talked to us so grandly," said Gretchen to Mrs. Woods one evening, "that I did not know half that he was saying; but it made me feel that I might be somebody, and I do intend to be. It is a good thing to have a teacher with great expectations."

"Yes," said Mrs. Woods, "when there is so little to expect. People don't take a lot of nothing and make a heap of something in this world. It is all like a lot of feathers thrown against the wind. *Nevertheless* it makes one happier to have prospects, if they are far away. I used to; but they never came to nothing, unless it was to bring me way out here."

The log school-house was a curious place. The children's benches consisted of split logs on pegs, without backs. The sides of the building were logs and sods, and the roof was constructed of logs and pine boughs. All of the children were barefooted, and several had but poor and scanty clothing. Yet the very simplicity of the place had a charm.

Benjamin sat alone, apart from the rest. It was plain to be seen that he was brooding over the painful event of the morning. Gretchen had grown cheerful again, but the bitter expression on the young Indian's face seemed to deepen in intensity. Mr. Mann saw it. To quiet his agitation, he began his teaching by going to him and sitting down beside him on the rude bench and opening to him the primer.

"You understand English?" said Mr. Mann.

"A little. I can talk Chinook."

In the Chinook vocabulary, which was originally the trade language of all the tribes employed by the Hudson Bay Company in collecting furs, most of the words resemble in sound the objects they represent. For example, a wagon in Chinook is chick-chick, a clock is ding-ding, a crow is kaw-kaw, a duck, quack-quack, a laugh, tee-hee; the heart is tum-tum, and a talk or speech or sermon, wah-wah. The language was of English invention; it took its name from the Chinook tribes, and became common in the Northwest. Nearly all of the old English and American traders in the Northwest learned to talk Chinook, and to teach Chinook was one of the purposes of the school.

"Can you tell me what that is?" asked Mr. Mann, pointing to the letter A in the primer.

"Fox-trap."

"No; that is the letter A."

"How do you know?"

Our digger of Greek roots from Cambridge was puzzled. He could not repeat the story of Cadmus to this druid of the forest or make a learned talk on arbitrary signs. He answered happily, however, "Wise men said so."

"Me understand."

"That is the letter B."

"Yes, aha! Boston tilicum, you let her be. Old woman no good; me punish her. Knock-sheet —stick her" (club her).

Mr. Mann saw at once the strange turn that the young Indian's mind had taken. He was puzzled again.

"No, Benjamin; I will teach you what to do."

"Teach me how to club her? You are good! Boston tilicum, we will be brothers—you and I. She wah-wah, but she is no good."

"That is C."

"Aha! *She* heap wah-wah, but *she* no good."

"Now, that is A, B, and that is C. Try to remember them, and I will come soon and talk with you again."

"You wah-wah?"

"Yes," said Mr. Mann, doubtful of the Indian's thought.

"She wah-wah?"

"Yes."

"You heap wah-wah. You good. She heap wah-wah. She no good. Potlatch come; dance. She wah-wah no more. I wah-wah."

Mr. Mann was pained to see the revengeful

trend of the Indian's thought. The hints of the evil intention of the Potlatch troubled him, but his faith in the old chief and the influence of his own integrity did not falter.

Gretchen was the most advanced scholar in the school. Her real mother had been an accomplished woman, and had taken great pains with her education. She was well instructed in the English branches, and had read five books of Virgil in Latin. Her reading had not been extensive, but it had embraced some of the best books in the English language. Her musical education had been received from a German uncle, who had been instructed by Herr Wieck, the father of Clara Schumann. He had been a great lover of Schumann's dreamy and spiritual music, and had taught her the young composer's pieces for children, and among them Romance and the Traumerei. He had taught her to play the two tone poems together in changing keys, beginning with the Traumerei and returning again to its beautiful and haunting strains. Gretchen interpreted these poems with all the color of true feeling, and under her bow they became enchantment to a musical ear and a delight to even as unmusical a soul as Mrs. Woods.

Gretchen's chief literary pleasure had been the

study of the German poets. She had a poetic mind, and had learned to produce good rhymes. The songs of Uhland, Heine, and Schiller delighted her She had loved to read the strange stories of Hoffman, and the imaginative works of Baron Fouqué. She used to aspire to be an author or poet, but these aspirations had received no countenance from Mrs. Woods, and yet the latter seemed rather proud to regard her ward as possessing a superior order of mind.

"If there is anything that I do despise," Mrs. Woods used to say, "it is books spun out of the air, all about nothin'! Dreams were made for sleep, and the day was made for work. I haven't much to be proud of in this world. I've always been a terror to lazy people and to Injuns, and if any one were to write my life they'd have some pretty stirring stories to tell. I have no doubt that I was made for something."

Although Mrs. Woods boasted that she was a terror to Indians, she had been very apprehensive of danger since the Whitman colony massacre. She talked bravely and acted bravely according to her view of moral courage, but with a fearful heart. She dreaded the approaching Potlatch, and the frenzy that calls for dark deeds if the dance of the evil spirits should conclude the approaching feast.

There was a sullen look in Benjamin's face as he silently took his seat in the log school-house the next morning. Mr. Mann saw it, and instinctively felt the dark and mysterious atmosphere of it. He went to him immediately after the opening exercises, and said:

"You haven't spoken to me this morning; what troubles you?"

The boy's face met the sympathetic eye of the master, and he said:

"I was happy on the morning when I came—sun; *she* hate Indian, talk against him to you; make me unhappy—shade; think I will have my revenge—*pil-pil;* then music make me happy; you make me happy; night come, and I think of her—she hate Indian—shade. Me will have my revenge—*pil-pil.* She say I have no right here; she have no right here; the land all belong to Umatilla; then to me; I no have her here. Look out for the October moon—Potlatch—dance—*pil-pil.*"

"I will be a friend to you, Benjamin."

"Yes, Boston tilicum, we will be friends."

"And I will teach you how to be noble—like a king. You felt good when I was kind to you?"

4

"Yes, Boston tilicum."

"And when the music played?"

"Yes, Boston tilicum."

"Then you must be good to her; that will make her feel good toward you. Do you see?"

There came a painful look into the young Indian's face.

"I good to her, make her good? She good to me make me good? She no good to me. She say I no right here. The land belong to Umatilla. She must go. You stay. Look out for the October moon. She wah-wah no more."

"It is noble to be good; it makes others good."

"Then why isn't *she* good? She make me ugly; you make me good. I think I will punish her—*pil-pil;* then you speak kind, and the music play, then I think I will punish her not. Then dark thoughts come back again; clouds come again; hawks fly. What me do? Me am two selves; one self when I think of you, one when I think of her. She say I have no right. She have no right. All right after Potlatch. I wah-wah; she wah-wah no more."

"Be good yourself, Benjamin. Be kind to her; make her kind. You do right."

The young Indian hesitated, then answered:

"I do as you say. You are friend. I'll do as I feel when the music play. I try. So you say."

The cloud passed. The teacher paid the Indian boy special attention that morning. At noon Gretchen played Von Weber's Wild Hunt of Lutzow, which drove Napoleon over the Rhine. The rhythm of the music picturing the heroic cavalry enchanted Benjamin, and he said: "Play it over again." After the music came a foot-race among the boys, which Benjamin easily won. The afternoon passed quietly, until in the cool, lengthening shadows of the trail the resolute form of Mrs. Woods appeared.

Benjamin saw her, and his calm mood fled. He looked up at the master.

"I is come back again—my old self again. She say I no business here; she no business here. She wah-wah."

The master laid his hand on the boy's shoulder kindly and bent his face on his.

"I do as you say," the boy continued. "I will not speak till my good self come again. I be still. No wah-wah."

He dropped his eyes upon a page in the book, and sat immovable. He was a noble picture of a struggle for self-control in a savage and untutored heart.

Mrs. Woods asked for Gretchen at the door, and the master excused the girl, thanking her for the music that had delighted the school at the noon-hour. As she was turning to go, Mrs. Woods cast a glance toward Benjamin, and said to the master in an undertone: "He's tame now—quiet as a purring cat. The cat don't lick cream when the folks are around. But he'll make trouble yet. An Injun is a Injun. I hate Injuns, though Parson Lee says I am all wrong. When you have seen as many of 'em as I have, you'll know more than you do now."

Benjamin did not comprehend the words, but he felt that the woman had said something injurious to him. The suspicion cut him to the quick. His black eye sparkled and his cheek burned. The scholars all seemed to be sorry at the impression that Mrs. Woods's muttered words had left in his mind. He had struggled for two days to do his best—to follow his best self.

School closed. Benjamin rose like a statue. He stood silent for a time and looked at the slanting sun and the dreamy afternoon glories of the glaciers, then moved silently out of the door. The old chief met him in the opening, and saw the hurt and troubled look in his face.

"What have you been doing to my boy?" he said to the master. "Has he not been good?"

"Very good; I like him," said Mr. Mann. "He is trying to be good here," pointing to his heart. "The good in him will grow. I will help him."

The old chief and the boy walked away slowly out of the shadows of the great trees and up the cool trail. The tall master followed them with his eye. In the departing forms he saw a picture of the disappearing race. He knew history well, and how it would repeat itself on the great plateau and amid the giant forests of the Oregon. He felt that the old man was probably one of the last great chiefs of the Umatillas.

On one of the peninsulas of the Oregon, the so-called Islands of the Dead, the old warriors of the tribes were being gathered by the plagues that had come to the territories and tribal regions ever since the Hudson Bay Company established its posts on the west of the mountains, and Astoria had been planted on the great river, and settlers had gathered in the mountain-domed valley of the Willamette. Wherever the white sail went in the glorious rivers, pestilence came to the native tribes. The Indian race was perceptibly vanishing. Only one son of seven was left to Umatilla. What would be the fate of this boy?

The master went home troubled over the event of the afternoon. He was asking the Indian to be better than his opponent, and she was a well-meaning woman and nominally a Christian.

His first thought was to go to Mrs. Woods and ask her to wholly change her spirit and manners, and, in fact, preach to her the same simple doctrine of following only one's better self that he had taught to the young prince. But he well knew that she had not a teachable mind. He resolved to try to reach the same result through Gretchen, whom she upbraided with her tongue but loved in her heart.

Mrs. Woods had come to regard it as her appointed mission to abuse people for their good. She thought it tended toward their spiritual progress and development. She often said that she felt "called to set things right, and not let two or three people have their own way in everything"—a view of life not uncommon among people of larger opportunities and better education.

Benjamin came to school the next morning silent and sullen, and the master went to him again in the same spirit as before.

"She say I no right here," he said. "She suffer for it. She wah-wah. Look out for the October moon."

"No, you are a better Indian now."

"Yes; sometimes."

"The better Indian harms no one—one's good self never does evil. You are to be your good self, and please me."

The young Indian was silent for a time. He at last said, slowly:

"But me know who will."

"Do what, Benjamin?"

"Make her suffer—punish."

"Who?"

"I know a bad Indian who will. He say so."

"You must not let him. You are son of a chief."

"I will try. I no wah-wah now."

At noon Benjamin was light-hearted, and led the sports and games. He was very strong, and one of his lively feats was to let three or four children climb upon his back and run away with them until they tumbled off. He seemed perfectly happy when he was making the others happy, and nothing so delighted him as to be commended. He longed to be popular, not from any selfish reason, but because to be liked by others was his atmosphere of contentment. He was kindly above most Indians, a trait for which his father was famous. He was even kindly above many of the white people.

The next morning he came to school in good humor, and a curious incident occurred soon after the school began. A little black bear ventured down the trail toward the open door, stopping at times and lifting up its head curiously and cautiously. It at last ventured up to the door, put its fore feet on the door-sill, and looked into the room.

"Kill it!" cried one of the boys, a recent emigrant, in the alarm. "Kill it!"

"What harm it do?" said the Indian boy. "Me drive it away."

The young Indian started toward the door as at play, and shook his head at the young bear, which was of the harmless kind so well known in the Northwest, and the bear turned and ran, while the Indian followed it toward the wood. The odd event was quite excusable on any ground of rule and propriety in the primitive school.

"It no harm; let it go," said the boy on his return; and the spirit of the incident was good and educational in the hearts of the school.

The charm of his life was Gretchen's violin. It transfigured him; it changed the world to him. His father was a forest philosopher; the boy caught a like spirit, and often said things that were a revelation to Mr. Mann.

"Why do you like the violin so much?" said the latter to him one day.

"It brings to me the thing longed for—the thing I long to know."

"Why, what is that?"

"I can't tell it—I feel it here—I sense it—I shall know—something better—yonder—the thing we long for, but do not know. Don't you long for it? Don't you feel it?"

The tall schoolmaster said "Yes," and was thoughtful. The poor Indian had tried to express that something beyond his self of which he could only now have a dim conception, and about which even science is dumb. Mr. Mann understood it, but he could hardly have expressed it better.

The boy learned the alphabet quickly, and began to demand constant attention in his eagerness to learn. Mr. Mann found that he was giving more than the allotted time to him. To meet the case, he appointed from time to time members of the school "monitors," as he called them, to sit beside him and help him.

One day he asked Gretchen to do this work. The boy was delighted to be instructed by the mistress of the violin, and she was as pleased with the honor of such monitorial duties to the son of a chief. But an unexpected episode grew out of all this mutual good-will and helpful kindness.

Benjamin was so grateful to Gretchen for the pains that she took with his studies that he wished to repay her. He had a pretty little Cayuse pony which he used to ride; one day after school he caused it to be brought to the school-house, and, setting Gretchen upon it, he led it by the mane up the trail toward her home, a number of the pupils following them. On the way the merry-making party met Mrs. Woods. She was as astonished as though she had encountered an elephant, and there came into her face a look of displeasure and anger.

"What kind of doings are these, I would like to know?" she exclaimed, in a sharp tone, standing in the middle of the way and scanning every face.

"Riding out with an Injun, Gretchen, are you? That's what you are doing. Girl, get off that horse and come with me! That is the kind of propriety that they teach out in these parts, is it? and the master came from Harvard College, too! One would think that this world was just made to enjoy one's self in, just like a sheep pasture, where the lambs go hopping and skipping, not knowing that they were born to be fleeced."

She hurried Gretchen away excitedly, and the school turned back. Benjamin was disappointed, and looked more hurt than ever before. On the way he met his old father, who had come out to look for him, and the rest of the scholars dispersed to their homes.

That evening, after a long, vivid twilight, such as throws its splendor over the mountain ranges in these northern latitudes, Mrs. Woods and Gretchen were sitting in their log-house just within the open door. Mr. Woods was at the block-house at Walla Walla, and the cabin was unprotected. The light was fading in the tall pines of the valleys, and there was a deep silence everywhere, undisturbed by so much as a whisper of the Chinook winds. Mrs. Woods's thoughts seemed far away — doubtless among the old meadows, orchards, and farm-fields of New England. Gretchen was playing the musical glasses.

Suddenly Mrs. Woods's thoughts came back from their far-away journeys. She had seen something that disturbed her. She sat peering into a tract of trees which were some three hundred feet high—one of the great tree cathedrals of the Northwestern forests. Suddenly she said:

"Gretchen, there are Injuns in the pines. Watch!"

Gretchen looked out, but saw nothing.

The shadows deepened.

"I have twice seen Injuns passing from tree to tree and hiding. Why are they there? There—look!"

A sinewy form in the shadows of the pines appeared and disappeared. Gretchen saw it.

"They mean evil, or they would not hide. Gretchen, what shall we do?"

Mrs. Woods closed the door and barred it, took down the rifle from the side of the room, and looked out through a crevice in the split shutter.

There was a silence for a time; then Mrs. Woods moved and said: "They are coming toward the house, passing from one tree to another. They mean revenge—I feel it—revenge on me, and Benjamin—he is the leader of it."

The flitting of shadowy forms among the pines grew alarming. Nearer and nearer they came, and more and more excited became Mrs. Woods's apprehensions. Gretchen began to cry, through nervous excitement, and with the first rush of tears came to her, as usual, the thought of her violin.

She took up the instrument, tuned it with nervous fingers, and drew the bow across the strings, making them shriek as with pain, and then drifted into the air the music of the Traumerei.

"Fiddling, Gretchen—fiddling in the shadow of death? I don't know but what you are right—that tune, too!"

The music trembled; the haunting strain quivered, rose and descended, and was repeated over and over again.

"There is no movement in the pines," said Mrs. Woods. "It is growing darker. Play on. It does seem as though that strain was stolen from heaven to overcome evil with."

Gretchen played. An hour passed, and the moon rose. Then she laid down the violin and listened.

"Oh, Gretchen, he is coming! I know that

form. It is Benjamin. He is coming alone. What shall we do? He is—right before the door!"

Gretchen's eye fell upon the musical glasses, which were among the few things that she had brought from the East and which had belonged to her old German home. She had tuned them early in the evening by pouring water into them, as she had been taught to do in her old German village, and she wet her fingers and touched them to the tender forest hymn:

"Now the woods are all sleeping."

"He has stopped," said Mrs. Woods. "He is listening—play."

The music filled the cabin. No tones can equal in sweetness the musical glasses, and the trembling nerves of Gretchen's fingers gave a spirit of pathetic pleading to the old German forest hymn. Over and over again she played the air, waiting for the word of Mrs. Woods to cease.

"He is going," said Mrs. Woods, slowly. "He is moving back toward the pines. He has changed his mind, or has gone for his band. You may stop now."

Mrs. Woods watched by the split shutter until

past midnight. Then she laid down on the bed, and Gretchen watched, and one listened while the other slept, by turns, during the night. But no footstep was heard. The midsummer sun blazed over the pines in the early morning; birds sang gayly in the dewy air, and Gretchen prepared the morning meal as usual, then made her way to the log school-house.

She found Benjamin there. He met her with a happy face.

"Bad Indian come to your cabin last night," said he. "He mean evil; he hate old woman. She wah-wah too much, and he hate. Bad Indian hear music—violin; he be pleased—evil hawks fly out of him. Good Indian come back. One is tied to the other. One no let the other go. What was that low music I hear? Baby music! Chinook wind in the bushes! Quail—mother-bird singing to her nest! I love that music.

"Say, you play at Potlatch, frighten away the hawks; mother-birds sing. No devil dance. Say, I have been good; no harm old wah-wah. Will you—will you play—play that tin-tin at Potlatch under the big moon?"

A great thought had taken possession of the young Indian's mind, and a great plan—one worthy of a leader of a peace congress. Gretchen saw the plan in part, but did not fully comprehend it. She could only see that his life had become a struggle between good and evil, and that he was now following some good impulse of his better nature.

CHAPTER IV.

MRS. WOODS'S TAME BEAR.

Mrs. Woods was much alone during this summer. Her husband was away from home during the working days of the week, at the saw and shingle mill on the Columbia, and during the same days Gretchen was much at school.

The summer in the mountain valleys of Washington is a long serenity. The deep-blue sky is an ocean of intense light, and the sunbeams glint amid the cool forest shadows, and seem to sprinkle the plains with gold-dust like golden snow. Notwithstanding her hard practical speech, which was a habit, Mrs. Woods loved Nature, and, when her work was done, she often made little journeys alone into the mountain woods.

In one of these solitary excursions she met with a little black cub and captured it, and, gathering it up in her apron like a kitten, she ran with it toward her cabin, after looking behind to see if the mother bear was following her. Had she seen the mother of the cunning little black creature in her apron pursuing her, she would have dropped the cub, which would have insured her escape from danger. But the mother bear did not make an early discovery of the loss in her family. She was probably out berrying, and such experiences of stolen children were wholly unknown to the bear family in Washington before this time. The Indians would not have troubled the little cub.

The black bear of the Cascades is quite harmless, and its cubs, like kittens, seem to have a sense of humor unusual among animals. For a white child to see a cub is to desire it to tame for a pet, and Mrs. Woods felt the same childish instincts when she caught up the little creature, which seemed to have no fear of anything, and ran away with it toward her home.

It was Saturday evening when she returned, and she found both Mr. Woods and Gretchen waiting to meet her at the door. They were surprised to see her haste and the pivotal turning of her head at times, as though she feared pursuit from some dangerous foe.

Out of breath, she sank down on the log that

served for a step, and, opening her apron cautiously, said:

"See here."

"Where did you get that?" said Mr. Woods.

"I stole it."

"What are you going to do with it?"

"Raise it."

"What for?"

"For company. I haven't any neighbors."

"But what do you want it for?"

"It is so cunning. It just rolled over in the trail at my feet, and I grabbed it and ran."

"But what if the mother-bear should come after it?" asked Gretchen.

"I would shoot her."

"That would be a strange way to treat your new neighbors," said Mr. Woods.

Mr. Woods put a leather strap around the neck of the little bear, and tied the strap to a log in the yard. The little thing began to be alarmed at these strange proceedings, and to show a disposition to use its paws in resistance, but it soon learned not to fear its captors; its adoption into the shingle-maker's family was quite easily enforced, and the pet seemed to feel quite at home.

There was some difficulty at first in teaching the

cub to eat, but hunger made it a tractable pupil of the berry dish, and Mrs. Woods was soon able to say:

"There it is, just as good as a kitten, and I would rather have it than to have a kitten. It belongs to these parts."

Poor Mrs. Woods! She soon found that her pet did "belong to these parts," and that its native instincts were strong, despite her moral training. She lost her bear in a most disappointing way, and after she supposed that it had become wholly devoted to her.

She had taught it to "roll over" for its dinner, and it had grown to think that all the good things of this world came to bears by their willingness to roll over. Whenever any member of the family appeared at the door, the cub would roll over like a ball, and expect to be fed, petted, and rewarded for the feat.

"I taught it that," Mrs. Woods used to say. "I could teach it anything. It is just as knowing as it is cunning, and lots of company for me out here in the mountains. It thinks more of me than of its old mother. You can educate anything."

As the cub grew, Mrs. Woods's attachment to

it increased. She could not bear to see its freedom restrained by the strap and string, and so she untied the string from the log and let it drag it about during the day, only fastening it at night.

"There is no danger of its running away," said she; "it thinks too much of me and the berry dish. I've tamed it completely; it's as faithful to its home as a house-cat, and a great deal more company than a cat or dog or any other dumb animal. The nicest bird to tame is a blue-jay, and the best animal for company is a cub. I do believe that I could tame the whole race of bears if I only had 'em."

Mrs. Woods had a pet blue-jay that she had taken when young from its nest, and it would do many comical things. It seemed to have a sense of humor, like a magpie, and to enjoy a theft like that bird. She finally gave it the freedom of the air, but it would return at her call for food and eat from her hand. The blue-jay is naturally a very wild bird, but when it is tamed it becomes very inquisitive and social, and seems to have a brain full of invention and becomes a very comical pet. Mrs. Woods called her pet bear Little Roll Over.

One day a visitor appeared at the emigrant's cabin. A black she-bear came out of the woods, and, seeing the cub, stood up on her haunches in surprise and seemed to say, "How came you here?" It was evidently the mother of the cub.

The cub saw its mother and rolled over several times, and then stood up on its haunches and looked at her, as much as to say, "Where did you come from, and what brought you here?" In the midst of this interesting interview Mrs. Woods appeared at the door of the cabin.

She saw the mother-bear. True to her New England instincts, she shook her homespun apron and said: "Shoo!"

She also saw that the little bear was greatly excited, and under the stress of temptation.

"Here," said she, "roll over."

The cub did so, but in the direction of its mother.

Mrs. Woods hurried out toward it to prevent this ungrateful gravitation.

The mother-bear seemed much to wonder that the cub should be found in such forbidden associations, and began to make signs by dipping her fore paws. The cub evidently understood these signs, and desired to renew its old-time family relations.

"Here," said Mrs. Woods, "you—you—you mind now; roll over—roll over."

In the midst of this interview Mrs. Woods appeared at the door of the cabin.

The cub did so, true to its education in one respect, but it did not roll in the direction of its foster-mother, but rolled toward its own mother. It turned over some five or more times, then bounded up and ran toward the she-bear. The latter dropped her fore feet on the earth again, and the two bears, evidently greatly delighted to find each other, quickly disappeared in the woods. As the cub was about to enter the bushes it turned and gave a final glance at Mrs. Woods and rolled over.

This was too much for Mrs. Woods's heart. She said:

"After all I have done for ye, too! Oh, Little Roll Over, Little Roll Over, I wouldn't have thought it of you!"

She surveyed the empty yard, threw her apron over her head, as stricken people used to do in Lynn in the hour of misfortune, and sat down on the log at the door and cried.

"I never have had any confidence in Injuns," she said, "since my saw walked off. But I did have some respect for bears. I wonder if I shall ever meet that little cre'tur' again, and, if I do, if it will roll over. This world is all full of disappointments, and I have had my share. Maybe I'll get it back to me yet. Nevertheless—"

Mrs. Woods often talked of Little Roll Over and its cunning ways; she hoped she would some time meet it again, and wondered how it would act if she should find it.

CHAPTER V.

THE NEST OF THE FISHING EAGLE.

BENJAMIN continued to attend the school, but it was evident that he did so with an injured heart, and chiefly out of love for the old chief, his father. He had a high regard for his teacher, whose kindness was unfailing, and he showed a certain partiality for Gretchen; but he was as a rule silent, and there were dark lines on his forehead that showed that he was unhappy. He would not be treated as an inferior, and he seemed to feel that he was so regarded by the scholars.

He began to show a peculiar kind of contempt for all of the pupils except Gretchen. He pretended not to see them, hear them, or to be aware of their presence or existence. He would pass through a group of boys as though the place was vacant, not so much as moving his eye from the direct path. He came and went, solitary and self-contained, proud, cold, and revengeful.

But this indifference was caused by sensitiveness and the feeling that he had been slighted. The dark lines relaxed, and his face wore a kindly glow whenever his teacher went to his desk—if the split-log bench for a book-rest might be so called. "I would give my life for Gretchen and you," he said one day to Mr. Mann; and added: "I would save them all for you."

There was a cluster of gigantic trees close by the school-house, nearly two hundred feet high. The trees, which were fir, had only dry stumps of limbs for a distance of nearly one hundred feet from the ground. At the top, or near the top, the green leaves or needles and dead boughs had matted together and formed a kind of shelf or eyrie, and on this a pair of fishing eagles had made their nest.

The nest had been there many years, and the eagles had come back to it during the breeding season and reared their young.

For a time after the opening of the school none of the pupils seemed to give any special attention to this high nest. It was a cheerful sight at noon to see the eagles wheel in the air, or the male eagle come from the glimmering hills and alight beside his mate.

One afternoon a sudden shadow like a falling cloud passed by the half-open shutter of the log school-house and caused the pupils to start. There was a sharp cry of distress in the air, and the master looked out and said:

"Attend to your books, children; it is only the eagle."

But again and again the same swift shadow, like the fragment of a storm-cloud, passed across the light, and the wild scream of the bird caused the scholars to watch and to listen. The cry was that of agony and affright, and it was so recognized by Benjamin, whose ear and eye were open to Nature, and who understood the voices and cries of the wild and winged inhabitants of the trees and air.

He raised his hand.

"May I go see?"

The master bowed silently. The boy glided out of the door, and was heard to exclaim:

"Look! look! the nest—the nest!"

The master granted the school a recess, and all in a few moments were standing without the door peering into the tall trees.

The long dry weather and withering sun had caused the dead boughs to shrink and to break beneath the great weight of the nest that rested upon them. The eagle's nest was in ruins. It had fallen upon the lower boughs, and two young half-fledged eaglets were to be seen hanging helplessly on a few sticks in mid-air and in danger of falling to the ground.

It was a bright afternoon. The distress of the two birds was pathetic, and their cries called about them other birds, as if in sympathy.

The eagles seldom descended to any point near the plain in their flight, but mounted, as it were, to the sun, or floated high in the air; but in their distress this afternoon they darted downward almost to the ground, as though appealing for help for their young.

While the school was watching this curious scene the old chief of the Umatillas came up the cool highway or trail, to go home with Benjamin after school.

The eagles seemed to know him. As he joined the pitying group, the female eagle descended as in a spasm of grief, and her wing swept his plume. She uttered a long, tremulous cry as she passed and ascended to her young.

"She call," said the old chief. "She call me."

"I go," said Benjamin, with a look at his father.

"Yes, go—she call. She call—the God overhead he call. Go!"

A slender young pine ran up beside one of the giant trees, tall and green. In a moment Benjamin was seen ascending this pine to a point where he could throw himself upon the smallest of the great trees and grasp the ladder of the lower dead branches. Up and up he went in the view of all, until he had reached a height of some hundred and fifty feet.

The eagles wheeled around him, describing higher circles as he ascended. He reached the young eagles at last, but passed by them. What was he going to do?

There was a shelf of green boughs above him, which would bear the weight of a nest. He went up to them at a distance of nearly two hundred feet. He then began to gather up the fallen sticks of the old nest, and to break off new sticks and to construct a new nest. The old chief watched him with pride, and, turning to the master, said:

"Ah-a—that is my boy. He be me. I was he once—it is gone now—what I was."

When Benjamin had made a nest he descended, and at the peril of his own life, on the decayed limbs, he rescued the two young eagles that were hanging with heads downward and open beaks. He carried them up to the new nest and placed them in it, and began to descend.

But a withered bough that he grasped was too slender for his weight, and broke. He grasped another, but that too gave way. He tried to drop into the top of the tall young pine below him, but, in his effort to get into position to do so, limb after limb of dead wood broke, and he came falling to the earth, amid the startled looks of the chief and the cries of the children.

The ground was soft, and his body lay for a time half imbedded in it.

He was senseless, and blood streamed from his nose and reddened his eyes. The old chief seized his arm and tried to raise him, but the effort brought no sign of life, and his body was lowered slowly back again by the agonized father, who sat down and dropped his head on his son's breast.

Mr. Mann brought water and wet the boy's lips and bathed his brow. He then placed his hand over the boy's heart and held it there. There was a long silence. The old chief watched the teacher's hand. He seemed waiting for a word of hope; but Mr. Mann did not speak.

The old chief lifted his head at last, and said, appealingly:

"Boston tilicum, you do not know how I feel! You do not know—the birds know—*you* do not know!"

The teacher rubbed the boy's breast and arms, and said:

"He will revive."

"What, Boston tilicum?"

"He will *live*."

"My boy?"

"Yes."

The dark face brightened. The old man clasped the boy's hand and drew it to his breast. The children attempted to brush the earth out of the young hero's dark, matted hair, but the old chief said, mysteriously:

"No touch him! he is mine."

At last a convulsive movement passed over the boy's body. The teacher again pressed his hand on the heart of his pupil, and he quickly exclaimed:

"It beats."

The fiery sun gleamed from the snowy mountains. There were cool murmurs of winds in the trees, and they sent forth a resinous odor into the air. The balm dropped down like a messenger of healing.

Presently the boy's eyes opened and gazed steadily into the blue air.

The eagles were wheeling about the trees. The boy watched them, as though nothing had passed. They were making narrowing circles, and at last each alighted on the new nest beside their young.

He turned his face slowly toward his father.

"Saved!" he said. "They are happy. I fell. Let's go."

He rose up. As he did so the male eagle rose from his nest and, uttering a glad scream, wheeled in the sky and made his way through the crimson haze toward the fishing grounds of the lower Columbia.

The chief's eye followed him for a time; then the old man turned a happy face on the schoolmaster and children and said:

"I know how he feels—the Manitou overhead—he made the hearts of all; yours—the birds—mine. He is glad!"

There was something beautiful and pathetic in the old chief's sense of the common heart and feeling of all conscious beings. The very eagles seemed to understand it; and Master Mann, as he turned away from the school-house that day, said to Gretchen:

"I myself am being taught. I am glad to learn all this large life. I hope that you will one day become a teacher."

Gretchen went home that afternoon with a glad heart. Benjamin did not return to the school again for several days, and when he came back it seemed to be with a sense of humiliation. He seemed to feel somehow that he ought not to have fallen from the tree.

The fourth of July came, and Master Mann had invited the school to come together on the holiday for patriotic exercises. He had one of the pupils read the Declaration of Independence on the occasion, and Gretchen played the President's March on the violin. He himself made an historical address, and then joined in some games out of doors under the trees.

He brought to the school-house that day an American flag, which he hung over the desk during the exercises. When the school went out to play he said:

"I wish I could hang the flag from a pole, or from the top of one of the trees."

Benjamin's face brightened.

"I will go," he said; "I will go *up*."

"Hang it on the eagle's nest," said one of the pupils. "The eagle is the national bird."

Mr. Mann saw that to suspend the national emblem from the eagle's nest would be a patriotic episode of the day, and he gave the flag to Benjamin, saying:

" Beware of the rotten limbs."

" I no woman," said Benjamin; and, waving the flag, he moved like a squirrel up the trees. He placed the flag on the nest, while the eagles wheeled around him, screaming wildly. He descended safely, and made the incident an object lesson, as Mr. Mann repeated the ode to the American eagle, found at that time in many reading-books.

While Mr. Mann was doing so, and had reached the line—

" Bird of Columbia, well art thou," etc.,

one of the eagles swept down to the nest and seized the banner in his talons. He rose again into the air and circled high, then with a swift, strong curve of the wings, came down to the nest again, and, seizing the flag, tore it from the nest and bore it aloft to the sky.

It was a beautiful sight. The air was clear, the far peaks were serene, and the glaciers of Mount Hood gleamed like a glory of crystallized light. The children cheered. The bird soared away in the blue heavens, and the flag streamed after him in

The eagle soared away in the blue heavens, and the flag streamed after him in his talons.

his talons. He dropped the flag at last over a dark, green forest. The children cheered again.

It was miles away.

"I go find it," said Benjamin; and he darted away from the place and was not seen until the next day, when he returned, bringing the flag with him.

Marlowe Mann never forgot that fourth of July on the Columbia.

CHAPTER VI.

THE MOUNTAIN LION.

One morning, as Mrs. Woods sat in her door picking over some red whortleberries which she had gathered in the timber the day before, a young cow came running into the yard, as if for protection. Mrs. Woods started up, and looked in the direction from which the animal had come running, but saw nothing to cause the alarm.

The cow looked backward, and lowed. Mrs. Woods set down her dish of red berries, took her gun, and went out toward the timber where the cow had been alarmed.

There was on the edge of the timber a large fir that the shingle-maker had felled when he first built his house or shack, but had not used, owing to the hardness of the grain. It lay on the earth, but still connected with its high stump, forming a kind of natural fence. Around it were beds of red phlox, red whortleberry bushes, and wild sunflowers.

The horny stump and fallen tree had been made very interesting to Mrs. Woods in her uneventful life by a white squirrel that often had appeared upon it, and made a pretty picture as it sat eating in the sun, its head half covered with its bushy tail. White squirrels were not common in the timber, and this was the only one that Mrs. Woods had ever seen.

"I wish that I could contrive to catch that there white squirrel," she said to Gretchen one day; "it would be a sight of company for me when you are gone. The bear used me mean, but I kind o' like all these little children of Natur'. But I don't want no Injuns, and no more bears unless *he* comes back again. The schoolmaster may like Injuns, and you may, but I don't. Think how I lost my saw; Injun and all went off together. I can seem to see him now, goin'."

As Mrs. Woods drew near the fallen tree she looked for the white squirrel, which was not to be seen. Suddenly the bushes near the stump moved, and she saw the most evil-looking animal that she had ever met drawing back slowly toward the fallen tree. It was long, and seemed to move more like an immense serpent than an animal. It had a cat-like face, with small ears and spiteful eyes, and a half-open mouth displaying a red tongue and sharp teeth. Its face was sly, malicious, cruel, and cowardly. It seemed to be such an animal as would attack one in the dark. It was much larger than a dog or common black bear.

Mrs. Woods raised her gun, but she thought that she was too far from the house to risk an encounter with so powerful an animal. So she drew back slowly, and the animal did the same defiantly. She at last turned and ran to the house.

"Gretchen," she said. "what do you think I have seen?"

"The white squirrel."

"No; a tiger!"

"But there are no tigers here; so the chief said."

"But I have just seen one, and it had the meanest-looking face that I ever saw on any living creature. It was all snarls. That animal is dangerous. I shall be almost afraid to be alone now."

"I shall be afraid to go to school."

"No, Gretchen, you needn't be afraid. I'll go with you mornin's and carry the gun. I like to walk mornin's under the trees, the air does smell so sweet."

That night, just as the last low tints of the long

twilight had disappeared and the cool, dewy airs began to move among the pines, a long, deep, fearful cry was heard issuing from the timber. Mrs. Woods started up from her bed and called, "Gretchen!"

The girl had been awakened by the cry, which might have been that of a child of a giant in pain.

"Did you hear that?" asked Mrs. Woods.

"Let's get up and go out," said Gretchen.

Presently the same long, clear, pitiable cry, as if some giant distress, was repeated.

"It seems human," said Mrs. Woods. "It makes me want to know what it is. Yes, let us get up and go out."

The cry was indeed pleading and magnetic. It excited pity and curiosity. There was a strange, mysterious quality about it that drew one toward it. It was repeated a third time and then ceased.

There was a family by the name of Bonney who had taken a donated claim some miles from the Woodses on the Columbia. They had two boys who attended the school.

Early the next morning one of these boys, named Arthur, came over to the Woodses in great distress, with a fearful story.

"Something," he said, "has killed all of our

cattle. They all lie dead near the clearing, just as though they were asleep. They are not injured, as we can see; they are not shot or bruised, nor do they seem to be poisoned—they are not swelled—they look as though they were alive—but they are cold—they are just dead. Did you hear anything in the timber last night?"

"Yes," said Mrs. Woods. "Wasn't it mysterious? Lost your cattle, boy? I am sorry for your folks. Mabbie (may be) 'tis Injuns."

"No; father says that he can find no injury on them."

"'Tis awful mysterious like," said Mrs. Woods, "cattle dyin' without anything ailin' 'em! I've always thought this was a good country, but I don't know. Tell your folks I'm sorry for 'em. Can I do anything for you? I'll come over and see ye in the course of the day."

That night the same strange, wild, pleading cry was repeated in the timber.

"There's something very strange about that sound," said Mrs. Woods. "It makes me feel as though I must run toward it. It draws me. It makes me feel curi's. It has haunted me all day, and now it comes again."

"Do you suppose that the cry has had anything

to do with the death of Mr. Bonney's cattle?" asked Gretchen.

"I don't know—we don't understand this country fully yet. There's something very mysterious about the death of those cattle. You ought to have seen 'em. They all lie there dead, as though they had just lost their breath, and that was all."

The next night was silent. But, on the following morning, a boy came to the school with a strange story. He had been driving home his father's cows on the evening before, when an animal had dropped from a great tree on the neck of one of the cows, which struggled and lowed for a few minutes, then fell, and was found dead. The boy and the other cattle had run away on the sudden appearance of the animal. The dead cow presented the same appearance as the cows of Mr. Bonney had done.

When the old chief appeared at the schoolhouse with Benjamin that morning, the school gathered around him and asked him what these things could mean. He replied, in broken Chinook, that there was a puma among them, and that this animal sucked the blood of its victims.

The puma or cougar or panther, sometimes spelled *painter*, is the American lion. It is commonly called the mountain lion in the Northwest. It belongs to the cat family, and received the name of lion from its tawny color. When its appetite for blood has been satisfied, and its face is in repose, it is a very beautiful animal; but when seeking its prey it presents a mean, cowardly, stealthy appearance, and its face is a picture of cruelty and evil. It will destroy as many as fifty sheep in a night, sucking their blood and leaving them as though they had died without any external injury. This terrible animal is easily tamed if captured young, and, strange to say, becomes one of the most affectionate and devoted of pets. It will purr about the feet and lick the hands of its master, and develop all the attractive characteristics of the domestic cat.

"We must have a puma-hunt," said the chief, "now—right away."

"Not to-day?" said the teacher.

"Yes," said the chief, "now—he eat your children. Find boy dead some day, just like cow. He drop down from a tree on a papoose. Benjamin and I will go hunt."

The two disappeared. For several days they did not return. But, one morning, a party of Indians in hunting-gear came riding up to the school-house, full of gay spirits and heroic pride.

The mountain lion.

Behind them came the old chief on foot, moving slowly, as though tired, and with him was Benjamin.

The Indian boy had a brown skin of an animal on his shoulder—a raw hide with very beautiful fur.

The old chief came into the school-room with an air of pride, and stood for a few minutes silent before the master. His face, though wrinkled, was really beautiful and noble, in the light of the happy intelligence that awaited communication. He at last looked each pupil in the face and then said:

"We have killed the puma. School no fear now."

He took the skin of the animal from Benjamin's shoulder, and held it up before the eyes of all.

"Boston tilicum, who killed the animal?" he said.

"It was you?" asked the teacher.

"No—not me, not me, no!"

"The braves?"

"No—not the braves. No." The old chief paused, and then said:

"Boston tilicum, it was Benjamin. Treat him well. He is good to me—he mean well. He likes you—he die for you. Tell the boys it was Benjamin."

He turned away slowly, with a bearing of pride. The Indian boy gave the puma's skin to the master, and took his seat in silence. There was a spirit in the strange scene that was touching, and the master's lip quivered as he took the old chief's hand that bright morning, as a parting sign of gratitude and good-will. He felt the innate brotherhood of all human hearts, and returned to his desk happy in his calling and work; and seeing that the natural rights of all men were secured; and that the human heart has the same impulses everywhere, as he had never seen these truths before.

That night Gretchen told the story of the puma to Mrs. Woods, who had learned the leading incidents of it in the afternoon as she came to meet the girl in the trail, on the way from school.

CHAPTER VII.

THE SMOKE-TALK.

ONE day in September Mrs. Woods was at work in her cabin, and Gretchen was at school. Mrs. Woods was trying to sing. She had a hard, harsh voice always, and the tune was a battle-cry. The hymn on which she was exercising her limited gifts was not one of the happy tunes of Methodism, which early settlers on the Columbia loved to sing. It was a very censorious rhyme and took a very despondent view of the human heart:

> "The pure testimony poured forth from the Spirit
>   Cuts like a two-edgèd sword;
> And hypocrites now are most sorely tormented
>   Because they're condemnèd by the Word."

She made the word "hypocrites" ring through the solitary log-cabin—she seemed to have the view that a large population of the world were of this class of people. She paused in her singing and looked out of the door.

"There's one honest woman alive," she remarked to herself. "Thank Heaven, *I* never yet feared the face of clay!"

A tall, dark form met her eye—a great shadow in the scintillant sunlight. It was an aged Indian, walking with a staff. He was coming toward the cabin.

"Umatilla!" she said. "What can he want of me?"

The old chief approached, and bowed and sat down on a log that answered for a door-step.

"I walk with a staff now," he said. "My bow has drifted away on the tide of years—it will never come back again. I am old."

"You have been a good man," said Mrs. Woods, yielding to an impulse of her better nature. She presently added, as though she had been too generous, "And there aren't many good Injuns—nor white folks either for that matter."

"I have come to have a smoke-talk with you," said the old chief, taking out his pipe and asking Mrs. Woods to light it. "Listen! I want to go home. When a child is weary, I take him by the hand and point him to the smoke of his wigwam. He goes home and sleeps. I am weary. The Great Spirit has taken me by the hand; he points to the smoke of the wigwam. There comes a time when all want to go home. I want to go home. Umatilla is going home. I have *not* spoken."

The smoke from his pipe curled over his white head in the pure, clear September air. He was eighty or more years of age. He had heard the traditions of Juan de Fuca, the Greek pilot, who left his name on the straits of the Puget Sea. He had heard of the coming of Vancouver in his boyhood, the English explorer who named the seas and mountains for his lieutenants and friends, Puget, Baker, Ranier, and Townsend. He had known the forest lords of the Hudson Bay Company, and of Astoria; had seen the sail of Gray as it entered the Columbia, and had heard the preaching of Jason Lee. The murder of Whitman had caused him real sorrow. Umatilla was a man of peace. He had loved to travel up and down the Columbia, and visit the great bluffs of the Puget Sea. He lived for a generation at peace with all the tribes, and now that he was old he was venerated by them all.

"You are a good old Injun," said Mrs. Woods, yielding to her better self again. "I don't say it about many people. I do think you have done your best—considering."

"I am not what I want to be," said Umatilla. "It is what we want to be that we shall be one day; don't you think so? The Great Spirit is going to make me what I want to be—he will make us all what we want to be. My desires are better than I —I will be my desires by and by. My staff is in my hand, and I am going home. The old warriors have gone home. They were thick as the flowers of the field, thick as the stars of the night. My boys are gone home—they were swift as the hawks in the air. Benjamin is left to the Umatillas. He is no butcher-bird; no forked tongue—he will remember the shade of his father. My heart is in his heart. I am going home. I have *not* spoken."

He puffed his pipe again, and watched an eagle skimming along on the great over-sea of September gold. The Indian language is always picturesque, and deals in symbols and figures of speech. It is picture-speaking. The Indians are all poets in their imaginations, like children. This habit of personification grows in the Indian mind with advancing years. Every old Indian speaks in poetic figures. Umatilla had not yet "spoken," as he said; he had been talking in figures, and merely approaching his subject.

There was a long pause. He then laid down his pipe. He was about to speak:

"Woman, open your ears. The Great Spirit lives in women, and old people, and little children. He loves the smoke of the wigwam, and the green fields of the flowers, and the blue gardens of stars. And he loves music—it is his voice, the whisper of the soul.

"He spoke in the pine-tops, on the lips of the seas, in the shell, in the reed and the war-drum. Then *she* came. He speaks through *her*. I want *her* to speak for me. My people are angry. There are butcher-birds among them. They hate you— they hate the cabin of the white man. The white men take away their room, overthrow their forests, kill their deer. There is danger in the air.

"The October moon will come. It will grow. It will turn into a sun on the border of the night. Then come Potlatch. My people ask for the Dance of the Evil One. I no consent—it means graves.

"Let me have *her* a moon—she play on the air. She play at the Potlatch for me. She stand by my side. The Great Spirit speak through her. Indians listen. They will think of little ones, they will think of departed ones, they will think of the hunt —they will see graves. Then the night will pass.

Then the smoke will rise again from white man's cabin. Then I die in peace, and go home to the Great Spirit and rest. Will you let me have her? I *have* spoken."

Mrs. Woods comprehended the figurative speech. The old chief wished to take Gretchen to his wigwam for a month, and have her play the violin on the great night of the Potlatch. He hoped that the influence of the music would aid him in preventing the Dance of the Evil Spirits, and a massacre of the white settlers. What should she say?

"I will talk with Gretchen," she said. "You mean well. I can trust you. We will see."

He rose slowly, leaning on his staff, and emptied his pipe. It required a resolute will now to cause his withered limbs to move. But his steps became free after a little walking, and he moved slowly away. Poor old chief of the Cascades! It was something like another Sermon on the Mount that he had spoken, but he knew not how closely his heart had caught the spirit of the Divine Teacher.

When Gretchen came home from school, Mrs. Woods told her what had happened, and what the old chief had asked.

Mr. Woods had returned from the block-houses.

He said: "Gretchen, go! Your *Traumerei* will save the colony. Go!"

Gretchen sat in silence for a moment. She then said: "I can trust Umatilla. I will go. I want to go. Something unseen is leading me—I feel it. I do not know the way, but I can trust my guide. I have only one desire, if I am young, and that is to do right. But is it right to leave you, mother?'

"Mother!" how sweet that word sounded to poor Mrs. Woods! She had never been a mother. Tears filled her eyes—she forced them back.

"Yes, Gretchen—go. I've always had to fight my way through the world, and I can continue to do so. I've had some things to harden my heart; but, no matter what you may do, Gretchen, I'll always be a mother to *you*. You'll always find the latch-string on the outside. You ain't the wust girl that ever was, if I did have a hand in bringing you up. Yes—go."

"Your heart is right now," said Gretchen; "and I want to speak to you about Benjamin. He told me a few days ago that he hated you, but that no one should ever harm you, because he loved the Master."

"He did, did he?" said Mrs. Woods, starting

up. "Well, I hate him, and I'll never forgive him for tellin' you such a thing as that."

"But, mother, don't you love *the* Master, and won't you be friendly and forgiving to Benjamin, for *his* sake? I wish you would. It would give you power; I want you to do so."

"I'll think about it, Gretchen. I don't feel quite right about these things, and I'm goin' to have a good talk with Father Lee. The boy has some good in him."

"I wish you would tell him that."

"Why?"

"Sympathy makes one grow so."

"That's so, Gretchen. Only praise a dog for his one good quality, and it will make a good dog of him. I 'spect 'tis the same with folks. But my nature don't break up easy. I shall come out right some time. I tell you I'm goin' to have a talk with Father Lee. It is his preachin' that has made me what I am, and may be I'll be better by and by."

Mrs. Woods, with all her affected courage, had good reason to fear an Indian outbreak, and to use every influence to prevent it. The very mention of the Potlatch filled her with recent terror. She well knew the story of the destruction of Whitman and a part of his missionary colony.

That was a terrible event, and it was a scene like that that the new settlers feared, at the approaching Potlatch; and the thought of that dreadful day almost weakened the faith of Mr. Mann in the Indians.

We must tell you the old-time history of the tragedy which was now revived in the new settlement.

THE CONJURED MELONS.

Most people who like history are familiar with the national story of Marcus Whitman's "Ride for Oregon"*—that daring horseback trip across the continent, from the Columbia to the Missouri, which enabled him to convince the United States Government not only that Oregon could be reached, but that it was worth possessing. Exact history has robbed this story of some of its romance, but it is still one of the noblest wonder-tales of our own or any nation. Monuments and poetry and art must forever perpetuate it, for it is full of spiritual meaning.

Lovers of missionary lore have read with delight the ideal romance of the two brides who agreed to cross the Rocky Mountains with their husbands,

---

* See Historical Notes.

Whitman and Spaulding; how one of them sang, in the little country church on departing, the whole of the hymn—

"Yes, my native land, I love thee,"

when the voices of others failed from emotion. They have read how the whole party knelt down on the Great Divide, beside the open Bible and under the American flag, and took possession of the great empire of the Northwest in faith and in imagination, and how history fulfilled the dream.

At the time of the coming of the missionaries the Cayuse Indians and Nez-Percés occupied the elbow of the Columbia, and the region of the musical names of the Wallula, the Walla Walla, and Waülaptu. They were a superstitious, fierce, and revengful race. They fully believed in witchcraft or conjuring, and in the power to work evil through familiar spirits. Everything to them and the neighboring tribes had its good or evil spirit, or both—the mountains, the rivers, the forest, the sighing cedars, and the whispering firs.

The great plague of the tribes on the middle Columbia was the measles. The disease was commonly fatal among them, owing largely to the manner of treatment. When an Indian began to show the fever which is characteristic of the disease, he was put into and inclosed in a hot clay oven. As soon as he was covered with a profuse perspiration he was let out, to leap into the cold waters of the Columbia. Usually the plunge was followed by death.

There was a rule among these Indians, in early times, that if the "medicine-man" undertook a case and failed to cure, he forfeited his own life. The killing of the medicine-man was one of the dramatic and fearful episodes of the Columbia.

Returning from the East after his famous ride, Whitman built up a noble mission station at Waülaptu. He was a man of strong character, and of fine tastes and ideals. The mission-house was an imposing structure for the place and time. It had beautiful trees and gardens, and inspiring surroundings.

Mrs. Whitman was a remarkable woman, as intelligent and sympathetic as she was heroic. The colony became a prosperous one, and for a time occupied the happy valley of the West.

One of the vices of the Cayuse Indians and their neighbors was stealing. The mission station may have overawed them for a time into seeming honesty, but they began to rob its gardens at last, and out of this circumstance comes a story, related to me by an old Territorial officer, which may be new to most readers. I do not vouch for it, but only say that the narrator of the principal incidents is an old Territorial judge who lives near the place of the Whitman tragedy, and who knew many of the survivors, and has a large knowledge of the Indian races of the Columbia. To his statements I add some incidents of another pioneer:

"The thieving Cayuses have made 'way with our melons again," said a young farmer one morning, returning from the gardens of the station. "One theft will be followed by another. I know the Cayuses. Is there no way to stop them?"

One of the missionary fraternity was sitting quietly among the trees. It was an August morning. The air was a living splendor, clear and warm, with now and then a breeze that rippled the leaves like the waves of the sea.

He looked up from his book, and considered the question half-seriously, half-humorously.

"I know how we used to prevent boys from stealing melons in the East," said he.

"How?"

"Put some tartar emetic in the biggest one. In the morning it would be gone, but the boys would never come after any more melons."

The young farmer understood the remedy, and laughed.

"And," added he, "the boys didn't have much to say about melons after they had eaten *that* one. The subject no longer interested them. I guess the Indians would not care for more than one melon of that kind."

"I would like to see a wah-wah of Indian thieves over a melon like that!" said the gardener. "I declare, I and the boys will do it!"

He went to his work, laughing. That day he obtained some of the emetic from the medical stores of the station, and plugged it into three or four of the finest melons. Next morning he found that these melons were gone.

The following evening a tall Indian came slowly and solemnly to the station. His face had a troubled look, and there was an air of mystery about his gait and attitude. He stopped before one of the assistant missionaries, drew together his blanket, and said:

"Some one here no goot. You keep a conjurer in the camp. Indian kill conjurer. Conjurer ought die; him danger, him no goot."

The laborers gathered round the stately Indian. They all knew about the nauseating melons, and guessed why he had come. All laughed as they heard his solemn words. The ridicule incensed him.

"You one conjurer," he said, "he conjure melons. One moon, two moons, he shall die."

The laborers laughed again.

"Half moon, more moons, he shall suffer—half moon, more moons," that is, sooner or later.

The missionary's face grew serious. The tall Indian saw the change of expression.

"Braves sick." He spread out his blanket and folded it again like wings. "Braves double up *so*"—he bent over, opening and folding his blanket. "Braves conjured; melon conjured—white man conjure. Indian kill him."

There was a puzzled look on all faces.

"Braves get well again," said the missionary, incautiously.

"Then you *know*," said the Indian. "You know—you conjure. Make sick—make well!"

He drew his blanket again around him and strode away with an injured look in his face, and vanished into the forests.

"I am sorry for this joke," said the missionary; "it bodes no good."

November came. The nights were long, and

there was a perceptible coolness in the air, even in this climate of April days.

Joe Stanfield, a half-breed Canadian and a member of Whitman's family, was observed to spend many of the lengthening evenings with the Cayuses in their lodges. He had been given a home by Whitman, to whom he had seemed for a time devoted.

Joe Lewis, an Indian who had come to Whitman sick and half-clad, and had received shelter and work from him, seems to have been on intimate terms with Stanfield, and the two became bitter enemies to the mission and sought to turn the Cayuses against it, contrary to all the traditions of Indian gratitude.

In these bright autumn days of 1847 a great calamity fell upon the Indians of the Columbia. It was the plague. This disease was the terror of the Northwestern tribes. The Cayuses caught the infection. Many sickened and died, and Whitman was appealed to by the leading Indians to stay the disease. He undertook the treatment of a number of cases, but his patients died.

The hunter's moon was now burning low in the sky. The gathering of rich harvests of furs had begun, and British and American fur-traders were seeking these treasures on every hand. But at the beginning of these harvests the Cayuses were sickening and dying, and the mission was powerless to stay the pestilence.

A secret council of Cayuses and half-breeds was held one night under the hunter's moon near Walla Walla, or else on the Umatilla. Five Crows, the warrior, was there with Joe Lewis, of Whitman's household, and Joe Stanfield, alike suspicious and treacherous, and old Mungo, the interpreter. Sitkas, a leading Indian, may have been present, as the story I am to give came in part from him.

Joe Lewis was the principal speaker. Addressing the Cayuses, he said:

"The moon brightens; your tents fill with furs. But Death, the robber, is among you. Who sends Death among you? The White Chief (Whitman). And why does the White Chief send among you Death, the robber, with his poison? That he may possess your furs."

"Then why do the white people themselves have the disease?" asked a Cayuse.

None could answer. The question had turned Joe Lewis's word against him, when a tall Indian arose and spread his blanket open like a wing. He stood for a time silent, statuesque, and thoughtful.

The men waited seriously to hear what he would say.

It was the same Indian who had appeared at the mission after the joke of the plugged melons.

"Brothers, listen. The missionaries are conjurers. They conjured the melons at Waülaptu. They made the melons sick. I went to missionary chief. He say, 'I make the melons well.' I leave the braves sick, with their faces turned white, when I go to the chief. I return, and they are well again. The missionaries conjure the melons, to save their gardens. They conjure you now, to get your furs."

The evidence was conclusive to the Cayuse mind. The missionaries were conjurers. The council resolved that all the medicine-men in the country should be put to death, and among the first to perish should be Whitman, the conjurer.

Such in effect was the result of the secret council or councils held around Waülaptu.

Whitman felt the change that had come over the disposition of the tribes, but he did not know what was hidden behind the dark curtain. His great soul was full of patriotic fire, of love to all men, and zeal for the gospel.

He was nothing to himself—the cause was

everything. He rode hither and thither on the autumn days and bright nights, engaged in his great work.

He went to Oregon City for supplies.

"Mr. McKinley," he said to a friend, "a Cayuse chief has told me that the Indians are about to kill all the medicine-men, and myself among them. I think he was jesting."

"Dr. Whitman," said McKinley, "a Cayuse chief never jests."

He was right. The fateful days wore on. The splendid nights glimmered over Mount Hood, and glistened on the serrated mountain tents of eternal snow. The Indians continued to sicken and die, and the universal suspicion of the tribes fell upon Whitman.

Suddenly there was a war-cry! The mission ran with blood. Whitman and his wife were the first to fall. Then horror succeeded horror, and many of the heroic pioneers of the Columbia River perished.

"The Jesuits have been accused of causing the murder of Whitman," said one historian of Washington to me. "They indignantly deny it. I have studied the whole subject for years with this opinion, that the Indian outbreak and its tragedies had its origin, and largely gathered its force, from the terrible joke of the conjured melons.

"That was the evidence that must have served greatly to turn the Indian mind against one of the bravest men that America has produced, and whose name will stand immortal among the heroes of Washington and Oregon."

I give this account as a local story, and not as exact history; but this tradition was believed by the old people in Washington.

When any one in the new settlement spoke of the Potlatch, this scene came up like a shadow. Would it be repeated?

CHAPTER VIII.

THE BLACK EAGLE'S NEST.

In the log school-house, Lewis and Clarke's Expedition was used as a reading-book. Master Mann had adopted it because it was easy to obtain, and served as a sort of local geography and history.

In this book is an account of a great black eagle's nest, on the Falls of the Missouri; and the incident seemed intensely to interest the picturesque mind of Benjamin.

"Let us go see," said Benjamin, one day after this poetic part of Lewis and Clarke's narrative had been read.

"What do you mean?" asked Mr. Mann.

"I carry canoe, and we go and find him!"

"What?"

"The black eagle's nest."

"Why?"

"I'll get a plume—wear it here. Please father. I love to please father."

There was to be a few weeks' vacation in a part of September and October, and Benjamin's suggestion led Mr. Mann to plan an excursion to the Falls of the Missouri at that time. The old chief would be glad to have Benjamin go with him and help hunt, and carry the canoe. They would follow the Salmon River out of the Columbia, to a point near the then called Jefferson River, and so pass the mountains, and launch themselves on the Missouri, whence the way would be easy to the Falls.

The dream of this expedition seemed to make Benjamin perfectly happy. He had already been over a part of this territory, with his father, on a visit to the friendly tribes.

The mid-autumn in the valleys of the Columbia and Missouri Rivers is serene, and yet kindles, with a sort of fiery splendor. The perfect days of America are here.

Master Mann and Benjamin started on their expedition with a few Indians, who were to see them to the Jefferson River and there leave them.

The Yankee schoolmaster had a prophetic soul, and he felt that he was treading the territory of future empires.

Launched on the Missouri, the thought of what the vast plains might become overwhelmed him at times, and he would lie silent in his boat, and pray and dream.

The soul of the Indian boy seemed as bright as the golden air of the cloudless days, during most of the time on the Salmon River, and while passing through the mountains. But he would sometimes start up suddenly, and a shade would settle on his face.

Master Mann noticed these sudden changes of mood, and he once said to him:

"What makes you turn sad, Benjamin?"

"Potlatch."

"But that is a dance."

"Hawks."

"I think not, Benjamin!"

"You do not know. They have a bitter heart. My father does not sleep. It is you that keeps him awake. He loves you; you love me and treat me well; he loves you, and want to treat you well—see. *She* make trouble. Indians meet at night—talk bitter. They own the land. They have rights. They threaten. Father no sleep. Sorry."

THE FALLS OF THE MISSOURI.

The Falls of the Missouri are not only wonderful and beautiful, but they abound with grand traditions. Before we follow our young explorer to the place, let us give you, good reader, some views of this part of Montana as it was and as it now appears.

We recently looked out on the island that once lifted the great black eagle's nest over the plunging torrent of water—the nest famous, doubtless, among the Indians, long before the days of Lewis and Clarke.

We were shown, in the city of Great Falls, a mounted eagle, which, it was claimed, came from this nest amid the mists and rainbows. The fall near this island, in the surges, is now known as the Black Eagle's Fall.

This waterfall has not the beauty or the grandeur of the other cataracts—the Rainbow Falls and the Great Falls—a few miles distant. But it gathers the spell of poetic tradition about it, and strongly appeals to the sense of the artist and the poet. The romancer would choose it for his work, as the black eagles chose it for their home.

Near it is one of the most lovely fountains in the world, called the Giant Spring.

> "Close beside the great Missouri,
> Ere it takes its second leap,
> Is a spring of sparkling water
> Like a river broad and deep."

The spring pours out of the earth near the fall in a great natural fountain, emerald-green, clear as crystal, bordered with water-cresses, and mingles its waters with the clouded surges of the Missouri. If a person looks down into this fountain from a point near enough for him to touch his nose to the water, all the fairy-like scenes of the Silver Springs and the Waukulla Spring in Florida appear. The royal halls and chambers of Undine meet the view, with gardens of emeralds and gem-bearing ferns. It kindles one's fancy to gaze long into these crystal caverns, and a practical mind could hardly resist here the poetic sense of Fouqué that created Undine.

The Black Eagle Falls, with its great nest and marvelous fountains, was a favorite resort of the Blackfeet Indians and other Indian tribes. It is related in the old traditions that the Piegans, on one of their expeditions against the Crows, rested here, and became enchanted with the fountain:

> "Hither came the warrior Piegans
> On their way to fight the Crow;
> Stood upon its verge, and wondered
> What could mean the power below."

The Piegans were filled with awe that the fountain rose and fell and gurgled, as if in spasms of pain. They sent for a native medicine-man.

"Why is the fountain troubled?" they asked.

"This," said the Indian prophet, "is the pure stream that flows through the earth to the sun. It asks for offerings. We cast the spoils of war into it, and it carries them away to the Sun's *tepee*, and the Sun is glad, and so shines for us all."

The Blackfeet worshiped the Sun. The Sun River, a few miles above this cataract, was a medicine or sacred river in the tribal days, and it was in this region of gleaming streams and thundering waterfalls that the once famous Sun-dances were held.

There was a barbarous splendor about these Sun-dances. The tribes gathered for the festival in the long, bright days of the year. They wore ornaments of crystal, quartz, and mica, such as would attract and reflect the rays of the sun. The dance was a glimmering maze of reflections. As it reached its height, gleaming arrows were shot into the air. Above them, in their poetic vision, sat the Sun in his *tepee*. They held that the thunder was caused by the wings of a great invisible bird. Often, at the close of the Sun-dance on the sultry days, the clouds would gather, and the thunder-bird would shake its wings above them and cool the air. Delightful times were these old festivals on the Missouri. At evening, in the long Northern twilights, they would recount the traditions of the past. Some of the old tales of the Blackfeet, Piegans, and Chippewas, are as charming as those of La Fontaine.

The Rainbow Falls are far more beautiful than those of the Black Eagle. They are some six miles from the new city of Great Falls. A long stairway of two hundred or more steps conducts the tourist into their very mist-land of rocks and surges. Here one is almost deafened by the thunder. When the sun is shining, the air is glorious with rainbows, that haunt the mists like a poet's dream.

The Great Fall, some twelve miles from the city, plunges nearly a hundred feet, and has a roar like that of Niagara. It is one of the greatest water-powers of the continent.

The city of Great Falls is leaping into life in a legend-haunted region. Its horizon is a borderland of wonders. Afar off gleam the Highwood Mountains, with roofs of glistening snow. Buttes (hills with level tops) rise like giant pyramids here and there, and one may almost imagine that he is in the land of the Pharaohs. Bench lands diversify the wide plains. Ranches and great flocks are everywhere; armies of cattle; creeks shaded with cottonwood and box-elder; birds and flowers; and golden eagles gleaming in the air. The Rockies wall the northern plains.

The Belt Mountain region near Great Falls is a wonder-land, like the Garden of the Gods in Colorado, or the Goblin Land near the Yellowstone. It would seem that it ought to be made a State park. Here one fancies one's self to be amid the ruins of castles, cathedrals, and fortresses, so fantastic are the shapes of the broken mountain-walls. It is a land of birds and flowers; of rock roses, wild sunflowers, golden-rods; of wax-wings, orioles, sparrows, and eagles. Here roams the stealthy mountain lion.

This region, too, has its delightful legends.

One of these legends will awaken great curiosity as the State of Montana grows, and she seems destined to become the monarch of States.

In 1742 Sieur de la Verendrye, the French

Governor of Quebec, sent out an expedition, under his sons and brother, that discovered the Rocky Mountains, which were named *La Montana Roches*. On the 12th of May, 1744, this expedition visited the upper Missouri, and planted on an eminence, probably in the near region of Great Falls, a leaden plate bearing the arms of France, and raised a monument above it, which the Verendryes named *Beauharnois*. It is stated that this monument was erected on a river-bluff, between bowlders, and that it was twenty feet in diameter.

There are people who claim to have discovered this monument, but they fail to produce the leaden plate with the arms of France that the explorers buried. The search for this hidden plate will one day begin, and the subject is likely greatly to interest historical societies in Montana, and to become a very poetic mystery.

Into this wonder-land of waterfalls, sun-dances, and legends, our young explorers came, now paddling in their airy canoe, now bearing the canoe on their backs around the falls.

Mr. Mann's white face was a surprise to the native tribes that they met on the way, but Benjamin's brightness and friendly ways made the journey of both easy.

They came to the Black Eagle Falls. The great nest still was there. It was as is described in the book of the early explorers.

It hung over the mists of the rapids, and, strangely enough, there were revealed three black plumes in the nest.

Benjamin beheld these plumes with a kind of religious awe. His eyes dilated as he pointed to them.

"They are for me," he said. "One for me, one for father, and one for you. I'll get them all."

He glided along a shelf of rocks toward the little island, and mounted the tree. The black eagles were yet there, though their nest was empty. He passed up the tree under the wings of the eagles, and came down with a handful of feathers.

"The book was true," said he.

They went to Medicine River, now called the Sun River, and there witnessed a Sun-dance.

It was a scene to tempt a brilliant painter or poet. The chiefs and warriors were arrayed in crystals, quartz, and every bright product of the earth and river that would reflect the glory of the sun.

They returned from where the city of Great Falls is now, back to the mountains and to the tributaries of the Columbia. Benjamin appeared before his father, on his return, with a crest of black eagle's plumes, and this crest the young Indian knight wore until the day of his death.

"I shall wear mine always," he said to his father. "You wear yours."

"Yes," said his father, with a face that showed a full heart.

"Both together," said Benjamin.

"Both together," replied Umatilla.

"Always?" said Benjamin.

"Always," answered the chief.

The Indians remembered these words. Somehow there seemed to be something prophetic in them. Wherever, from that day, Umatilla or Young Eagle's Plume was seen, each wore the black feather from the great eagle's nest, amid the mists and rainbows or mist-bows of the Falls of the Missouri.

It was a touch of poetic sentiment, but these Indian races of the Columbia lived in a region that was itself a school of poetry. The Potlatch was sentiment, and the Sun-dance was an actual poem. Many of the tents of skin abounded with picture-writing, and the stories told by the night fires were full of picturesque figures.

Gretchen's poetic eye found subjects for verse in all these things, and she often wrote down her impressions, and read them to practical Mrs. Woods, who affected to ignore such things, but yet seemed secretly delighted with them.

"You have *talons*," she used to say, "but they don't amount to anything, anyway. Nevertheless—"

The expedition to the Falls of the Missouri, and the new and strange sights which Benjamin saw there, led him to desire to make other trips with the schoolmaster, to whom he became daily more and more attached. In fact, the Indian boy came to follow his teacher about with a kind of jealous watchfulness. He seemed to be perfectly happy when the latter was with him, and, when absent from him, he talked of him more than of any other person.

In the middle of autumn the sky was often clouded with wild geese, which in V-shaped flocks passed in long processions overhead, *honking* in a trumpet-like manner. Sometimes a flock of snowy geese would be seen, and the laughing goose would be heard.

"Where do they go?" said Mr. Mann one day to Benjamin.

The boy told him of a wonderful island, now known as Whidby, where there were great gatherings of flocks of geese in the fall.

"Let's go see," said he. "The geese are thicker than the bushes there—the ponds are all alive with them there—honk—honk—honk! Let's go see."

"When the school is over for the fall we will go," said Mr. Mann.

The Indian boy's face beamed with delight. He dreamed of another expedition like that to the wonderful Falls. He would there show the master the great water cities of the wild geese, the emigrants of the air. The thought of it made him dance with delight.

Often at nightfall great flocks of the Canada geese would follow the Columbia towards the sea. Benjamin would watch them with a heart full of anticipation. It made him supremely happy to show the master the wonderful things of the beautiful country, and the one ambition of his heart now was to go to the lakes of the *honks*.

CHAPTER IX.

GRETCHEN'S VISIT TO THE OLD CHIEF OF THE CASCADES.

"Go to the chief's lodge, Gretchen, and stay until the Potlatch, and I will come to visit you." Such were the words of Mrs. Woods, as her final decision, after long considering the chief's request.

The forest lodge of the old chief of the Cascades was picturesque without and within. Outwardly, it was a mere tent of skins and curious pictography, under the shadows of gigantic trees, looking down on the glistening waters of the Columbia; inwardly, it was a museum of relics of the supposed era of the giant-killers, and of the deep regions of the tooth and claw; of Potlatches, masques and charms of *medas* and *wabenoes;* of curious pipes; of odd, curious feathers, and beautiful shells and feather-work and pearls. But, though all things here were rude and primitive, the old chief had a strong poetic sense, and the place and the arrangement of everything in it were very picturesque in its effect, and would have delighted an artist. On a hill near were grave-posts, and a sacred grove, in which were bark coffins in trees. Near by was an open field where the Indian hunters were accustomed to gather their peltries, and where visiting bands of Indians came to be hospitably entertained, and feasts were given *à la mode de sauvage*. From the plateau of the royal lodge ran long forest trails and pathways of blazed trees; and near the opening to the tent rose two poles, to indicate the royal rank of the occupant. These were ornamented with ideographic devices of a historical and religious character.

The family of Umatilla consisted of his squaw, an old woman partly demented, and Benjamin, who was now much of the time away with the schoolmaster.

The old chief was very kind to his unfortunate wife, and treated her like a child or a doll. Benjamin was about to take as his bride an Indian girl whom the English called Fair Cloud, and she was a frequent visitor at the tent.

To this patriarchal family Gretchen came one day, bringing her violin. Fair Cloud was there to receive her, and the crazy old squaw seemed to be made happy by the sight of her white face, and she did all that she could in her simple way to make her welcome. She gave her ornaments of shells, and pointed out to her a wabeno-tree, in whose tops spirits were supposed to whisper, and around which Indian visitors sometimes danced in the summer evenings.

The Indian maid was eager to hear the violin, but the old chief said: "It is the voice of the Merciful; let it be still—the god should not speak much."

He seemed to wish to reserve the influence of the instrument for the Potlatch, to make it an object of wonder and veneration for a time, that its voice might be more magical when it should be heard.

There was a kind of tambourine, ornamented with fan-like feathers, in the lodge. Fair Cloud used to play upon it, or rather shake it in a rhythmic way. There was also a war-drum in the lodge, and an Indian called Blackhoof used to beat it, and say:

> "I walk upon the sky,
> My war-drum 'tis you hear;
> When the sun goes out at noon,
> My war-drum 'tis you hear!

> "When forkèd lightnings flash,
>   My war-drum 'tis you hear.
> I walk upon the sky,
>   And call the clouds; be still,
>   My war-drum 'tis you hear!"

The tribes of the Oregon at this time were numerous but small. They consisted chiefly of the Chinooks, Vancouvers, the Walla Wallas, the Yacomars, the Spokans, the Caynses, the Nez-Percés, the Skagits, the Cascades, and many tribes that were scarcely more than families. They were for the most part friendly with each other, and they found in the Oregon or Columbia a common fishing-ground, and a water-way to all their territories. They lived easily. The woods were full of game, and the river of salmon, and berries loaded the plateaus. Red whortleberries filled the woodland pastures and blackberries the margins of the woods.

The climate was an almost continuous April; there was a cloudy season in winter with rainy nights, but the Japanese winds ate up the snows, and the ponies grazed out of doors in mid-winter, and spring came in February. It was almost an ideal existence that these old tribes or families of Indians lived.

Among the early friends of these people was

An Indian village on the Columbia.

Dick Trevette, whose tomb startles the tourist on the Columbia as he passes Mamaloose, or the Island of the Dead. He died in California, and his last request was that he might be buried in the Indian graveyard on the Columbia River, among a race whose hearts had always been true to him.

The old chief taught Gretchen to fish in the Columbia, and the withered crone cooked the fish that she caught.

Strange visitors came to the lodge, among them an Indian girl who brought her old, withered father strapped upon her back. The aged Indian wished to pay his last respects to Umatilla.

Indians of other tribes came, and they were usually entertained at a feast, and in the evening were invited to dance about the whispering tree.

The song for the reception of strangers, which was sung at the dance, was curious, and it was accompanied by striking the hand upon the breast over the heart at the words " Here, here, here ":

> " You resemble a friend of mine,
> A friend I would have in my heart—
> Here, here, *here*.

> " My heart is linked to thine;
> You are like a friend of mine—
> Here, here, *here*.

"Are we not brothers, then;
    Shall we not meet again—
        Here, here, *here ?*

"Mi, yes, we brothers be,
    So my fond heart sings to thee—
        Here, here, *here.*

"Ah! yes, we brothers be;
    Will you not answer me—
        Here, here, *here ?*"

Gretchen was happy in the new kind of life. She did not fear the Indians; in fact, the thing that she feared most was the promised visit of Mrs. Woods. She was sure that her foster-mother's spirit would change toward the Indians, but the change had not yet come.

One evening the schoolmaster came to call. He was bent upon a mission, as always. The family gave him a seat outside of the tent, and gathered around him, and they talked until the stars came out and were mirrored in the Columbia.

One of the first questions asked by the old chief was, "Is Eagle's Plume (Benjamin) brave?" (a good scholar).

"Yes, brave at times; he must learn to be brave always. He must always keep his better self. The world would be good if people would learn to keep their better selves. Do you see?"

"Yes."

"A chief should conquer himself first; obey the will of the Great Maniton—do you see?"

"Yes, but how can we know his will?"

"It is his will that we be our best minds. Forgive, and so make bad people good, and return good for bad. Do you see?"

"Yes, boy, do you see?" (to Benjamin).

"Yes, yes, I see what white man means. But white man do not so. He cheat—he kill."

"*Boston tilicum*, what do you say?" asked the chief.

"White man does not follow his best heart when he cheats and kills. It is wrong. All men should be brothers—see?"

"Yes, I have tried to be a brother. I have no shed blood—I live in peace—like yonder river. The stars love to shine on the peaceful river. Benjamin will learn. I go away when the swallows go, and no more come when the swallows bring the spring on their wings again. Teach Benjamin to be his good self all the time; make him good *here*."

All the Indian visitors who came to the place examined the violin cautiously, and the Indian hunters seemed to regard Gretchen with suspicion.

When any asked her to play for them, the old chief would answer: "Not now, but at the Potlatch—then it speak and you will hear; you will hear what it says."

But, of all the people that came to the lodge, no one could have been more curious than Mrs. Woods. She had been living in terror of the threatened events of the October feast, and yet she wished to make the Indians believe that she was indifferent to their ill-will, and that she possessed some hidden power that gave her security.

She approached the lodge slowly on the occasion of her visit, picking red whortleberries by the way. Benjamin watched her nervous motions, and felt that they implied a want of respect, and he grew silent and looked stoical. Gretchen went out to meet her, and brought her to the old chief.

It was a beautiful day, one of those long dreams of golden splendor that glorify the banks of the Oregon. Eccentric Victor Trevette and his Indian wife were at the lodge, and the company were joined by the Rev. Jason Lee, who had come up the Columbia in the interests of the mission in the Willamette Valley. Seattle* was there, from the

---

* See Historical Notes.

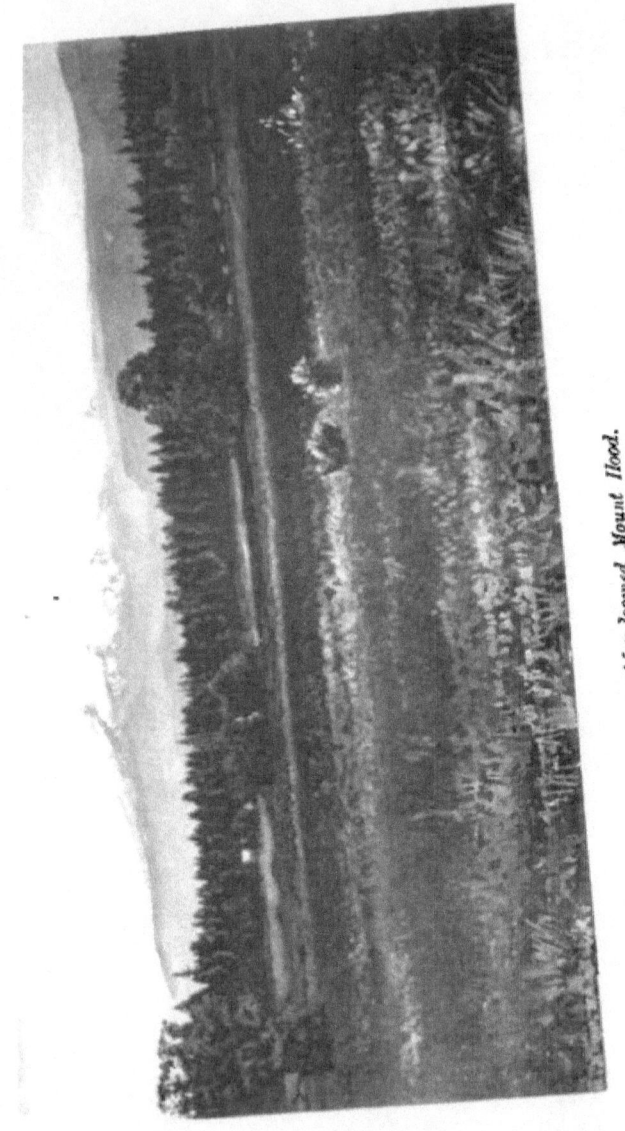

Afar loomed Mount Hood.

Willamette, then young, and not yet the titular chief of Governor Stevens.* It was a company of diverse spirits—Trevette, the reputed gambler, but the true friend of the Indian races; Lee, who had beheld Oregon in his early visions, and now saw the future of the mountain-domed country in dreams; sharp-tongued but industrious and warm-hearted Mrs. Woods; the musical German girl, with memories of the Rhine; and the Indian chief and his family. The Columbia rolled below the tall palisades, the opposite bank was full of cool shadows of overhanging rocks, sunless retreats, and dripping cascades of glacier-water. Afar loomed Mount Hood in grandeur unsurpassed, if we except Tacoma, inswathed in forests and covered with crystal crowns. The Chinook winds were blowing coolly, coming from the Kuro Siwo, or placid ocean-river from Japan; odoriferous, as though spice-laden from the flowery isles of the Yellow Sea. Warm in winter, cool in summer, like the Gulf winds of Floridian shores, the good angel of the Puget Sea territories is the Chinook wind from far Asia, a mysterious country, of which the old chief and his family knew no more than of the blessed isles.

"It is a day of the Great Manitou," said the old

---

* See Historical Notes.

chief. "He lights the sun, and lifts his wings for a shadow, and breathes on the earth. He fills our hearts with peace. I am glad."

"I only wish my people in the East knew how wonderful this country is," said Jason Lee. "I am blamed and distrusted because I leave my mission work to see what great resources here await mankind. I do it only for the good of others—something within me impels me to do it, yet they say I neglect my work to become a political pioneer. As well might they censure Joshua."

"As a missionary," said the old hunter, "you would teach the Indians truth; as a pioneer, you would bring colonies here to rob them of their lands and rights. I can respect the missionary, but not the pioneer. See the happiness of all these tribal families. Benjamin is right—Mrs. Woods has no business here."

"Adventurer," said Mrs. Woods, rising upon her feet, "I am a working-woman—I came out here to work and improve the country, and you came here to live on your Injun wife. The world belongs to those who work, and not to the idle. It is running water that freshens the earth. Husband and I built our house with our own hands, and I made my garden with my own hands, and I have defended my property with my own hands against bears and Injuns, and have kept husband to work at the block-house to earn money for the day of trouble and helplessness that is sure some day to come to us all. I raise my own garden-sass and all other sass. I'm an honest woman, that's what I am, and have asked nothing in the world but what I have earned, and don't you dare to question my rights to anything I possess! I never had a dollar that I did not earn, and that honestly, and what is mine is mine."

"Be careful, woman," said the hunter. "It will not be yours very long unless you have a different temper and tongue. There are black wings in the sky, and you would not be so cool if you had heard the things that have come to my ears."

Mrs. Woods was secretly alarmed. She felt that her assumed boldness was insincere, and that any insincerity is weakness. She glanced up a long ladder of rods or poles which were hung with Potlatch masks—fearful and merciless visages, fit to cover the faces of crime. She had heard that Umatilla would never put on a mask himself, although he allowed the custom at the tribal dances. Mrs. Woods dropped her black eyes from the ominous masks to the honest face of the chief.

"There," said she, lifting her arm, "there sits an honest man. He never covered his heart with a mask—he never covered his face with a mask. He has promised me protection. He has promised to protect the school. I can trust a man who never wears a mask. Most people wear masks—Death takes the masks away; when Death comes to Umatilla, he will find great Umatilla only, fearless and noble—honest and true, but no mask. He never wore a mask."

"But, woman," said Umatilla, "you are wearing a mask; you are afraid."

"Yes, but I can trust your word."

"You seek to please me for your own good."

"Yes—but, Umatilla, I can trust your word."

"The word of Umatilla was never broken. Death will come to Umatilla for his mask, and will go away with an empty hand. I have tried to make my people better.—Brother Lee, you have come here to instruct me—I honor you. Listen to an old Indian's story. Sit down all. I have something that I would say to you."

The company sat down and listened to the old chief. They expected that he would speak in a parable, and he did. He told them in Chinook the story of

THE WOLF BROTHER.

An old Indian hunter was dying in his lodge. The barks were lifted to admit the air. The winds of the seas came and revived him, and he called his three children to him and made his last bequests.

"My son," he said, "I am going out into the unknown life whence I came. Give yourself to those who need you most, and always be true to your younger brother."

"My daughter," he said, "be a mother to your younger brother. Give him your love, or for want of it he may become lonely and as savage as the animals are."

The two older children promised, and the father died at sunset, and went into the unknown life whence he came.

The old Indian had lived apart from the villages of men for the sake of peace; but now, after his death, the oldest son sought the villages and he desired to live in them. "My sister," he said, "can look out for my little brother. I must look out for myself."

But the sister tired of solitude, and longed to go to the villages. So one day she said to her little brother: "I am going away to find our brother who has taken up his abode in the villages. I will come back in a few moons. Stay you here."

But she married in the villages, and did not return.

The little brother was left all alone, and lived on roots and berries. He one day found a den of young wolves and fed them, and the mother-wolf seemed so friendly that he visited her daily. So he made the acquaintance of the great wolf family, and came to like them, and roam about with them, and he no longer was lonesome or wished for the company of men.

One day the pack of wolves came near the villages, and the little boy saw his brother fishing and his sister weaving under a tree. He drew near them, and they recognized him.

"Come to us, little brother," said they, sorry that they had left him to the animals.

"No—no!" said he. "I would rather be a wolf. The wolves have been kinder to me than you.

> "My brother,
> My brother,
> I am turning—
> I am turning
> Into a wolf.
>   You made me so!

> "My sister,
> My sister,
> I am turning—
> I am turning
> Into a wolf.
> You made me so!"

"O little brother, forgive me," said the sister; "forgive me!"

"It is too late now. See, I *am* a wolf!"

He howled, and ran away with the pack of wolves, and they never saw him again.

"Jason Lee, be good to my people when I am gone, lest they become like the little brother.

"Victor Trevette, be good to my people when I am gone, lest they become like the little brother."

The tall form of Marlowe Mann now appeared before the open entrance of the lodge. The Yankee schoolmaster had been listening to the story. The old chief bent his eye upon him, and said, "And, Boston tilicum, do you be good to Benjamin when I am gone, so that he shall not become like the little brother."

"You may play, Gretchen, now—it is a solemn hour; the voices of the gods should speak."

Gretchen took her violin. Standing near the door of the tent, she raised it to her arm, and the strains of some old German music rose in the glimmering air, and drifted over the Columbia.

"I think that there are worlds around this," said the old chief. "The Great Spirit is good."

The sun was going down. High in the air the wild fowls were flying, with the bright light yet on their wings. The glaciers of Mount Hood were flushed with crimson—a sea of glass mingled with fire. It was a pastoral scene; in it the old history of Oregon was coming to an end, after the mysteries of a thousand years, and the new history of civilization was beginning.

Evening came, and the company dispersed, but the old chief and Gretchen sat down outside of the tent, and listened to the murmuring music of the Dalles of the Columbia, and breathed the vital air. The Columbia is a mile wide in some places, but it narrows at the Dalles, or shelves and pours over the stone steps the gathered force of its many tides and streams. Across the river a waterfall filled the air with misty beauty, and a castellated crag arose solitary and solemn—the remnant of some great upheaval in the volcanic ages.

The red ashes of the sunset lingered after the fires of the long day had gone down, and the stars came out slowly. The old chief was sad and thoughtful.

A castellated crag arose solitary and solemn.

"Sit down by my feet, my child," he said to Gretchen, or in words of this meaning. "I have been thinking what it is that makes the music in the violin. Let us talk together, for something whispers in the leaves that my days are almost done."

"Let me get the violin and play to you, father; we are alone."

"Yes, yes; get the music, child, and you shall play, and we will talk. You shall sit down at my feet and play, and we will talk. Go, my little spirit."

Gretchen brought her violin, and sat down at his feet and tuned it. She then drew her bow, and threw on the air a haunting strain.

"Stop there, little spirit. It is beautiful. But what made it beautiful?"

"My bow—don't you see?"

Gretchen drew her bow, and again lifted the same haunting air.

"No—no—my girl—not the bow—something behind the bow."

"The strings?"

"No—no—something behind the strings."

"My fingers—so?"

"No—no—something behind the fingers."

"My head—*here?*"

"No—something behind that."

"My heart?"

"No—no—something behind that."

"I?"

"Yes—you, but something behind that. I have not seen it, my girl—your spirit. It is that that makes the music; but there is something behind that. I can feel what I can not see. I am going away, girl—going away to the source of the stream. Then I will know everything good is beautiful—it is good that makes you beautiful, and the music beautiful. It is good that makes the river beautiful, and the stars. I am going away where all is beautiful. When I am gone, teach my poor people."

Gretchen drew his red hand to her lips and kissed it. The chief bent low his plumed head and said:

"That was so beautiful, my little spirit, that I am in a haste to go. One moon, and I will go. Play."

Gretchen obeyed. When the strain died, the two sat and listened to the murmuring of the waters, as the river glided down the shelves, and both of them felt that the spirit of Eternal Goodness with a Father's love watched over everything.

The old chief rose, and said again:

"When I am gone to my fathers, teach my poor people." He added: "The voice of the good spirits ask it—the All-Good asks it—I shall go away—to the land whence the light comes. You stay—teach. You will?"

"Yes," said Gretchen—a consciousness of her true calling in life coming upon her, as in an open vision—"I will be their teacher."

The old chief seemed satisfied, and said: "It is well; I am going away.

Much of the chief's talk was acted. If he wished to speak of a star, he would point to it; and he would imitate a bird's call to designate a bird, and the gurgle of water when speaking of a running stream. He spoke Chinook freely, and to see him when he was speaking was to learn from his motions his meaning.

CHAPTER X.

MRS. WOODS MEETS LITTLE ROLL OVER AGAIN.

ONE day Rev. Jason Lee came up from the Cascades, in a boat, to visit Mr. and Mrs. Woods on their donation claim. Mr. Lee at this time was inspired with missionary zeal for the Indians, and he remembered Mrs. Woods kindly as an ignorant but earnest and teachable woman, whom the influence of his preaching had brought to his spiritual flock. He knew her needs of counsel and help, he pitied her hard and lonely life, and he came to visit her from time to time.

He had once given her a copy of Wesley's Hymns, and these hymns she had unconsciously learned, and delighted to quote on all occasions. Her favorite hymn in the collection was written by Thomas Olivers, one of Wesley's coadjutors, beginning—

"The God of Abrah'm praise."

She used to sing it often about her work; and one approaching the cabin, might often have heard her trying to sing to the old Hebrew melody of *Leoniel*—a tune perhaps as old as the Jewish Temple itself—such sublime thoughts as these—

> "The God of Abrah'm praise,
>   At whose supreme command
> From earth I rise, and seek the joys
>   At his right hand;
> I all on earth forsake,
>   Its wisdom, fame, and power;
> And him my only portion make,
>   My shield and tower.
>
> "He by himself hath sworn,
>   I on his oath depend;
> I shall, on eagles' wings upborne,
>   To heaven ascend:
> I shall behold his face,
>   I shall his power adore,
> And sing the wonders of his grace
>   Forever more."

Another favorite hymn, in an easy metre, was John Wesley's triumphant review of life in his middle age. The tune, although marked in the music-books C. P. M., and thus indicating some difficulty, was really as simple as it was lively, and carried the voice along like the music of a meadow stream:

"How happy is the pilgrim's lot,
   How free from every anxious thought,
      From worldly hope and fear!
   Confined to neither court nor cell,
   His soul disdains on earth to dwell—
      He only sojourns here."

Mrs. Woods was singing as usual about her work, when Jason Lee rapped at her door.

"Father Lee," said Mrs. Woods, "can I trust my eyes!—come again to see me, away out here in the timber? Well, you are welcome. I have got something on my mind, and I have long been wanting to have a talk with you. How is the mission at the Dalles?"

"It is prospering, but I regard it as my duty to leave it and go back to the East; and this may be my farewell visit, though I expect to come back again."

"Why, Father Lee, what has changed your mind? You surely can not think it your duty to leave this great country in the Oregon! You are needed here if anywhere in this world."

"Yes, but it is on account of this country on the Oregon being great, as you call it, that I must go away. It was once my calling in life to become a missionary to the Indians of Oregon, and to see this wonderful land. The same Voice that called me to that work calls me again to go back to tell the people of the East of their great opportunity here. I owe it to my country's future to do this. I have eaten the grapes of a promised land, and I must return to my own people with the good report. I believe that the best life of America will yet be here—it seems to be so revealed to me. My mission was to the Indians; it is now to induce colonies to come to the Oregon."

"Well, each heart knows its own calling and duty, and none of us are led alike. Father Lee, Gretchen has been reprovin' me, though she shouldn't, perhaps, being a girl. She was sassy to me, but she meant well. She is a well-meanin' girl, though I have to be hard on her sometimes—it is my duty to be, you know.

"Well, some months ago, more than a year, an Injun ran away with my best saw, and that gave me a prejudice against the Injuns, I suppose. Afterward, Young Eagle's Plume—Benjamin, the chief's boy—insulted me before the school by takin' a stick out of my hand, and I came to dislike him, and he hates me. There are many Injuns in the timber now, and they all cast evil looks at me whenever I meet them, and these things hint that they are goin' to capture me at the Potlatch and carry me away. I hate Injuns.

"But Gretchen has told me a thing that touches my feelin's. She says that Benjamin he says that he will protect me on account of his love for the master; and that, on account of my love for the good Master of us all and his cause, I ought to show a different spirit toward the Injuns. What do you think?"

"Gretchen is right, although a girl should be modest with her elders. Hatred only multiplies itself; when one overcomes his evil passions he gains others, and loses nothing. Do you see?"

"But I am always good to those I like and those who treat me well. Think how I used to take care of the sick folk on our way out here, and what I have tried to do for Gretchen!"

"'If ye love them that love you, what thank have ye?' All people love those who love them— the savages do. To give up one's evil desires, and to help others by returning love for hate, is the true life. The best friends in the world that we can have are those that we have drawn to our hearts by forgiveness. Do something good to every Indian that hates you, and you will never be carried away captive."

"But Whitman, remember Whitman: he showed the right spirit, and the Injuns killed *him!*"

"His death was caused by a misapprehension, and it made him a martyr. His work lives. Men live in their work."

"Well, Father Lee, if Benjamin can overcome his evil feelin's for his master, I ought to do so for mine, as Gretchen says. My bad spirit in this matter has long troubled me; it has caused a cloud to come over me when singin' hymns. I will give it all up now—I will give up everything, and just follow the better spirit. I want to do right, so that I can sing hymns."

When Father Lee left the cabin, Mrs. Woods accompanied him to his boat on the river.

As they were passing along under the tall spruces whose tops glimmered in the sun, and whose cool shadows made the trail delightful and refreshing, a black she-bear suddenly rose up before them, and a cub started up by her side. The great bear and the little bear both stood on their haunches, with their fore-feet outstretched like arms, as in great surprise. Mrs. Woods stopped and threw up her arms, and Parson Lee drew back.

Mrs. Woods looked at the little bear, and the little bear at her.

"Roll over, roll over!" she suddenly exclaimed. A strange event followed, very strange indeed in the eyes of the startled missionary. The little bear rolled itself into a ball, and began to turn over and over, and to come toward them in its somersaults.

The mother bear made a peculiar noise, dropped upon her four feet and ran off into the timber; and the little one, hearing the noise and movement, leaped up and followed her.

"What *does* that mean?" asked the missionary, in astonishment.

"That is Little Roll Over. I taught him that trick myself. He was once a pet of mine, and he ran away."

"Extraordinary!" said the missionary; "and it seems to me, if you have such a good influence over bears, you might do a great deal of good among the Indians."

"And I will," said Mrs. Woods. "I mean to live so I can sing hymns, and feel right about it."

On the return home, Mrs. Woods looked everywhere for her pet bear. She did not fear the old bear, for these animals are generally harmless if unmolested. She called, "Roll Over! Roll Over!" when she came to the place where she had had the adventure. But there was no answer except from the blue jays that piped out their shrill call in the tall trees.

Mrs. Woods came home to have a long battle with herself. Her idea of happiness seemed to be the freedom to sing hymns with a clear conscience, and the poor pioneer woman's philosophy was not very far from right.

CHAPTER XI.

MARLOWE MANN'S NEW ROBINSON CRUSOE.

BESIDES the Narrative of Lewis and Clarke, which was used in the school as a reader, Mr. Mann made use of another book in his teaching which greatly delighted his pupils and often awakened their sympathies. It was called "John R. Jewett and Thompson." It presented a picture of life on the coast early in the century. The strange story was much as follows:

THE ROBINSON CRUSOE OF VANCOUVER.

About the year 1802 the ship Boston, from Boston, Mass., went to Hull, England, to secure a cargo of goods to carry to the Indians on the Northwest coast of America to trade for furs. She was a general trading-vessel, such as roamed the seas of the world adventurously at that time, and often made fortunes for the merchants of New York, Boston, and other Atlantic port cities.

She was commanded by Captain John Salter, a clever man and a natural story-teller, whose engaging pictures of travel were sure to fascinate the young.

While in England this man met a lad by the name of John Rogers Jewett, who listened eagerly to his romantic adventures, and who desired to embark with him for America, and was allowed by his parents to make the voyage. The ship sailed around Cape Horn to Nootka Island, one of the islands on the west coast of Vancouver Island between the forty-ninth and fiftieth parallel. Here the whole crew, with the exception of young Jewett and a man by the name of Thompson, were massacred by the Indians, and the strange and tragic narrative of the survivors was an American and English wonder-tale seventy years ago. Mr. Jewett published the account of his capture and sufferings, under the title of "John R. Jewett and Thompson," or, to copy the title of the quaint old book before me, "A Narrative of the Adventures and Sufferings of John R. Jewett, only Survivor of the Crew of the Ship Boston, during a Captivity of nearly Three Years among the Savages of Nootka Sound." The book was issued from London, England, and from Middletown, Conn. After Robinson Crusoe, perhaps no book was more eagerly read by our grandfathers in their boyhood than this.

The Indian king of Nootka was Maquina. He used to visit the ship, sometimes wearing a wooden mask over his face representing some wild beast. Such masks are still to be found among the Indians of Vancouver.

Maquina was at first very friendly to Captain Salter, but one day the latter offended him, and he resolved to have his revenge by killing him and the crew, and destroying the ship. Accordingly, one morning, after he had been capering on deck and blowing a rude whistle, he said to the captain:

"When do you intend to sail?"

"To-morrow," replied the captain.

"You love salmon—much in Friendly Cove; go, then, and catch some," said the chief.

The captain thought it very desirable to have a large supply of fish on board, so he assented to the chief's proposal, and, after dinner with the latter, he sent away a jolly-boat or yawl with nine men to fish in Friendly Cove.

A series of tragedies followed. "I went down to my vise-bench in the steerage," says Mr. Jewett, in his Narrative, "where I was employed in cleaning muskets. I had not been there more than an hour, when I heard a great bustle and confusion on deck. I ran up the steerage stairs, but scarcely was my head above deck when I was caught by the hair by one of the savages. My hair was short, and I fell from his hold into the steerage. As I was falling, he struck me with an axe and cut a deep gash in my forehead. I remained in a state of suspense for some time, when Maquina himself appeared at the hatch and ordered me to come up. What a terrific spectacle met my eyes! Six naked savages stood in a circle around me, covered with the blood of my murdered comrades! I thought that my last moment had come, and commended my soul to my Maker.

"'John,' said the chief, 'I speak—you no say no; you say no—daggers come. Will you become my slave and fight for me?' I answered, 'Yes.' Then he told me that he would spare my life.

"Taking me by the hand, he led me to the quarter-deck, where the most horrid sight presented itself; the heads of our unfortunate captain and his crew, to the number of twenty-five, were arranged in a line.

"Maquina then ordered me to get the ship under way for Friendly Cove. We were there received by the inhabitants of the village with loud shouts of joy and a horrible drumming of sticks upon the roofs and sides of their houses. Maquina took me on shore to his house."

Young Jewett became a favorite of the chief's son, and was made a member of the tribe. He was compelled to marry an Indian princess, and his search for his wife is a wonderful romance, and really very poetic, as the marriage customs of the tribes are associated with a rustic festival worthy of a painter and poet. The young princess chosen was beautiful, and served him with the most affectionate devotion, but he could not love her, because he had been compelled to marry her.

The most remarkable incidents of this strange narrative are associated with the fate of those who were engaged in the massacre of the officers and crew of the Boston, and which show that the experience of retribution is a law common to all peoples and lands.

The principal chief or sub-chief among the warriors was Tootooch. He had married Maquina's sister. He ranked next to Maquina in all things pertaining to war, and he had been the foremost leader and the most merciless of conquerors in the destruction of the Boston. He killed two men on shore, presumably with his own hand.

Insanity is not common among the Indians. But a terrible mania took possession of this ambitious warrior. "While in the enjoyment of the highest health," says Mr. Jewett, "he was suddenly seized with delirium, in which he fancied that he saw the ghosts of the two men that he had murdered." The avenging vision followed him wherever he went. He was filled with terror at all times, and at last refused to eat to sustain his life. The Indians forced food into his mouth.

Maquina was informed of the terrible state of the warrior's mind by his sister, Tootooch's wife. He went to the haunted man's house, taking Mr. Thompson and Mr. Jewett with him. "We found him raving about the two murdered men, Hall and Wood," says Jewett. "Maquina placed provisions before him, but he would not eat."

At last the distressed *tyee*, induced by hunger, put forth his hand to touch the food. But he suddenly drew it back, saying that Hall and Wood were there.

"They will not let me eat," said he, with a look of despair and terror.

Maquina pointed to Thompson and Jewett.

"Is it they who have bewitched you?" he asked.

"*Wik* (no); John *klashish* (is good), Thompson *klashish* (is good)."

He arose and piteously put his hand on Jewett's shoulder, and, pointing to the food offered him, he said, " Eat."

" Eat it yourself," replied Mr. Jewett. " Hall and Wood are not there."

" You can not see them," he answered; " I can. I know that you can not see them."

" What do you do in your own country in such cases as this?" asked Maquina.

" We confine the person and whip him," said Jewett.

The chief ordered that the haunted warrior should be confined and whipped; but the pain did not relieve the warrior's mind of the terrible vision of the two men that he had killed. He grew more wild. He would torture his slaves for diversion. His wife fled from him. The vision continued until he became completely exhausted, and Death came with a merciful face.

" Early in June," says Mr. Jewett, " Tootooch, the crazy chief, died. The whole village set up a loud cry. The body was laid on a plank, and the head bound with a red fillet. It was then wrapped in an otter-skin robe and placed in a large coffin, which was ornamented with rows of white shells. It was buried by night in a cavern."

The *tyees* or chiefs had discussed often the policy of putting Mr. Jewett and Mr. Thompson to death, and so end all evidence of the destruction of the Boston in the event of new ships appearing on the coast. But the spectacle of Tootooch staring at the ghosts of the men that he had killed, and wasting away amid days and nights of horror, made them fear that the other warriors engaged in the massacre would become affected in the like way, and deterred them from any further violence. Jewett was at last rescued by a trading-ship, and was taken to the Columbia River, where he arrived shortly after the visit of Lewis and Clarke, of the famous expedition that bears these names. He finally came to New England and settled in Middletown, Conn. His history gives a very picturesque view of the habits and customs of the Indians on the Northwest coast nearly a century ago. The book can be found in antiquarian libraries, and should be republished in the interest of American folk-lore. The truth of the incidents gives the whole narrative a vivid and intense interest; it reads like De Foe.

CHAPTER XII.

OLD JOE MEEK AND MR. SPAULDING.

One day a man in a buckskin habit came to the door of the school-house and looked in upon the school. His face was that of a leader of men, hard and powerful; one could see that it feared nothing, and that it looked with contempt on whatever was artificial, affected, or insincere. His form had the strength and mettle of a pioneer. He rapped a loud, hard rap, and said, in a sturdy tone:

"May I come in?"

The master welcomed him cordially and courteously, and said:

"This is Mr. Meek, I believe?"

"Yes, old Joe Meek, the pioneer—you have heard of me."

"Yes, yes," said Mr. Mann. "You have caught the spirit of Oregon—you are Oregon. You have made the interest of this great country your life; I honor you for it. I feel the same spirit coming

OLD JOE MEEK AND MR. SPAULDING. 163

over me. What we do here is done for a thousand years, for here the great life of the Anglo-Saxon race is destined to come. I can see it; I feel it. The morning twilight of time is about me. I can hear the Oregon calling—calling; to teach here is a glorious life; the whole of humanity is in it. I have no wish to return to the East again."

"Stranger, give me your hand."

The New England schoolmaster took the hard hand of the old pioneer, and the two stood there in silence.

The children could not understand the great, soul-expanding sympathy that made these two men friends. They gazed on Mr. Meek's buckskin jacket and trousers with curiosity, for they were picturesque with their furs, belts, and weapons, and he looked like a warrior or a forest knight clad in armor.

He wore the same buckskin suit when he appeared in Washington as the delegate to Congress from Oregon. It was at the time of Polk and Dallas, and not a person in Washington probably knew him when he made his appearance at the Congressional Hotel.

The people at the hotel stared at him as the children did now. He went into the great dining-room with the other Congressmen, but alone and unknown. The colored waiters laughed at him as he took his seat at the table.

The other people at the table were served, but no one came near him. At last he turned and faced a hurrying colored man, and, in a voice that silenced the room, said:

"Waiter, come here!"

The waiter rolled up his eyes and said, "Sir?"

"Have you any big meat to-day?"

"Yes, sir."

"Any bear?"

"Any bear? bear? No, sir."

"Any buffalo?"

"Any buffalo—buffalo? Where did you come from? No, sir."

"Well, waiter you may bring me what you have."

The waiter went away with white teeth, and a smile and titter passed around the table. The waiter returned with the usual first course of the meal, and was about to hurry away, when the old pioneer took out his pistol and laid it down on the table, saying:

"Waiter, you stand there, I may want you; and if anybody wants to know who I am, tell him I am Hon. Joseph Meek, the delegate of the people of Oregon."

When it was known who Mr. Meek was, he was met by Mr. Dallas, the courtly Vice-President.

"I will attend you to the reception this afternoon, where you will meet the wives of the Congressmen," said he. "I will call for you at three."

The Vice-President called, and was surprised to find Mr. Meek still in his buckskins.

"You do not intend to go in that habit to the reception?" said he.

"Yes," said Mr. Meek, "or else not go at all. In the first place, I have nothing else to wear, and what is good enough for me to wear among the people of Oregon is good enough for their representative here."

We have given, in these two anecdotes, very nearly Mr. Meek's own words.

A few days after the visit of this most extraordinary man, another visitor came. She was an earnest-looking woman, on an Indian pony, and there was a benevolence in her face and manner that drew the whole school into immediate sympathy with her. The lady was Mrs. Spaulding, one of the so-called "Brides of Oregon." Her husband had come to the Territory with Dr. Whitman and his bride. The long missionary journey was the bridal tour of Mrs. Whitman and Mrs. Spaulding. They were the first white women who crossed the Rocky Mountains. It was related of Mrs. Spaulding, who had a beautiful voice, and was a member of a church quartet or choir in a country town in New York, as a leading singer, that, just before leaving the place for her long horseback journey of more than two thousand miles, she sang in the church the hymn beginning—

"Yes, my native land, I love thee,"

in such an affecting manner as to silence the rest of the choir, and melt the congregation to tears:

"Home, thy joys are passing lovely,
  Joys no stranger's heart can tell;
Happy scenes and happy country,
  Can I bid you all farewell?
    Can I leave thee,
  Far in heathen lands to dwell?"

This lady addressed the school, and spoke feelingly of the condition of the Indian race, and of the field for the teacher in the valleys of the Columbia.

Gretchen listened to the address with open heart. There are moments of revelation when a knowledge of one's true calling in life comes to the soul. Faith as a blind but true guide vanishes, and the eye sees. Such was the hour to Gretchen. She had often felt, when playing on the violin, that the inspiration that gave such influence to her music should be used in teaching the tribes that were so suscepible to its influence. This feeling had grown in the playing and singing of a school-song, the words of which were written by Mrs. Hunter, an English lady, and the wife of the famous Dr. Hunter, which showed the heroism and fortitude of the Indian character:

> "The sun sets at night and the stars shun the day,
> But glory remains when the light fades away;
> Begin, ye tormentors, your threats are in vain,
> For the son of Alknoomook will never complain."

The tune or melody was admirably adapted to the violin. Benjamin loved to hear it sung, and Gretchen was pleased to sing and to play it.

Mr. Mann asked Gretchen to play for Mrs. Spaulding, and she chose this simple but expressive melody. He then asked the school to sing, and he selected the words of

> "Yes, my native land, I love thee,"

to the music of Rousseau's Dream. Mrs. Spaulding could hardly keep from joining in the tune and hymn, then well known to all the missionary pioneers. At the words—

> "In the desert let me labor,
> On the mountain let me tell,"

her beautiful voice rose above the school, and Gretchen's fingers trembled as she played the air.

As the lady rode away, Gretchen felt tears coming into her eyes. The school was dismissed, and the pupils went away, but Gretchen lingered behind. She told Benjamin to go to the lodge, and that she would follow him after she had had a talk with the master.

"That song is beautiful," said Gretchen. "'In the desert let me labor.' That is what I would like to do all my life. Do you suppose that I could become a teacher among the Indians like Mrs. Spaulding? It would make me perfectly happy if I could. If I were to study hard, would you help me to find such a place in life?"

Gretchen's large eyes, filled with tears, were bent earnestly on the face of Mr. Mann.

"Yes," he said, "and if I can inspire you only to follow me in such work, it will repay me for an unknown grave in the forests of the Columbia."

Gretchen started; she trembled she knew not

why, then buried her face in her arms on the rude log desk and sobbed.

She raised her head at last, and went out, singing—

"In the desert let me labor."

It was a glorious sundown in autumn. The burning disk of the sun hung in clouds of pearl like an oriel-window in a magnificent temple. Black shadows fell on the placid waters of the Columbia, and in the limpid air under the bluffs Indians fished for salmon, and ducks and grebes sported in river weeds.

Marlowe Mann went away from the log schoolhouse that night a happy man. He had seen that his plans in life were already budding. He cared little for himself, but only for the cause to which he devoted his life—to begin Christian education in the great empire of Oregon.

But how unexpected this episode was, and how far from his early dreams! His spirit had inspired first of all this orphan girl from the Rhine, who had been led here by a series of strange events. This girl had learned faith from her father's prayers. On the Rhine she had never so much as heard of the Columbia—the new Rhine of the sundown seas.

CHAPTER XIII.

A WARNING.

One evening, as Gretchen was sitting outside of the lodge, she saw the figure of a woman moving cautiously about in the dim openings of the fir-trees. It was not the form of an Indian woman— its movement was mysterious. Gretchen started up and stood looking into the darkening shadows of the firs. Suddenly the form came out of the clearing—it was Mrs. Woods. She waved her hand and beckoned to Gretchen, and then drew back into the forest and disappeared.

Gretchen went toward the openings where Mrs. Woods had so suddenly and strangely appeared. But no one was there. She wondered what the secret of the mysterious episode could be. She returned to the lodge, but said nothing about what she had seen. She passed a sleepless night, and resolved to go to see her foster-mother on the following day.

So, after school the next afternoon, she returned to her old home for a brief visit, and to gain an explanation of the strange event of the evening before.

She found Mrs. Woods very sad, and evidently troubled by some ominous experience.

"So you saw me?" was her first salutation. "I didn't dare to come any further. They did not see me—did they?"

"But, mother, why did you go away—why did you come to the lodge?"

"O Gretchen, husband has been at home from the shingle-mill, and he has told me something dreadful!"

"What, mother?"

"There's a conspiracy!"

"Where?"

"Among the Injuns. A friendly Injun told husband in secret that there would be no more seen of the log school-house after the Potlatch."

"Don't fear, mother; the chief and Benjamin will protect that."

"But that isn't all, Gretchen. Oh, I am so glad that you have come home! There are dark shadows around us everywhere. I can feel 'em—can't you? The atmosphere is all full of dark faces and evil thoughts. I can't bear to sleep alone here now. Gretchen, there's a plot to capture the schoolmaster."

"Don't fear, mother. I know Umatilla—he will never permit it."

"But, Gretchen, the Injun told husband something awful."

"What?"

"That the schoolmaster would one day perish as Dr. Whitman did. Dr. Whitman was stricken down by the Injun whom he regarded as his best friend, and he never knew who dealt the blow. He went out of life like one smitten by lightning. O Gretchen!"

"But, mother, I do not fear. The Indians thought that Dr. Whitman was a conjurer. We make people true, the master says, by putting confidence in them. I believe in the old chief and in Benjamin, and there will no evil ever come to the schoolmaster or the log school-house."

"Gretchen, are you sure? Then I did not bring you away out here for nothing, did I? You may be the angel of deliverance of us all. Who knows? But, Gretchen, I haven't told you all yet."

Mrs. Woods's face clouded again.

"The Injun told husband that some of the warriors had formed a plot against *me*, and that, if they were to capture me, they would torture me. Gretchen, I am afraid. Don't you pity me?"

"Mother, I know my power over the chief and Benjamin, and I know the power of a chief's sense of honor. I do pity you, you are so distressed. But, mother, no evil will ever come to you where I am, nor the school where I am. I am going to be a teacher among these Indians, if I live; I feel this calling, and my work will somehow begin here."

"A teacher among the Injuns! You? You a teacher? Are anvils going to fly? Here I am, a poor lone woman, away out here three thousand miles from home, and tremblin' all over, at every sound that I hear at night, for fear I shall be attacked by Injuns, and you are dreamin', with your head all full of poetry, of goin' away and leavin' me, the best friend that you ever had on the earth, as good as a mother to you; of goin' away—of leavin' me, to teach a lot of savages! Gretchen, I knew that the world was full of empty heads, but I never realized how empty the human heart is until now! Been a mother to you, too!"

"O mother, I never thought of leavin' you unless you wished it."

"What did you think was goin' to become of me? I never kissed any child but you, and sometimes, when you are real good, I feel just as though I was your mother."

"I thought that you would help me."

"Help you, what doin'?"

"To teach the Indians."

"To teach the Injuns—Indians you call 'em! I'd like to teach one Injun to bring back my saw! I never tried to teach but one Injun—and he was *him*. You can't make an eagle run around a dooryard like a goose, and you can't teach an Injun to saw wood—the first thing you know, the saw will be missin'.—But how I am runnin' on! I do have a good deal of prejudice against the savages; nevertheless—"

"I knew, mother, that you would say 'nevertheless.' It seems to me that word is your good spirit. I wish you would tell me what thought came to your mind when you said that word."

"'Nevertheless?'"

"Yes."

"Well, the Master—"

"He said—"

"Yes—preach the gospel to every creature! I suppose that meant Injuns and all."

"Yes—he said '*teach*'—so the schoolmaster explained it."

"Did he? Well, I ought to obey it in spirit—hadn't I?—or at least not hinder others. I might help you teach it if I could get into the right spirit. But what put that thought into your head?"

"Mrs. Spaulding, the missionary, has been to visit the school. She sang so beautifully! These were the words:

"'In the desert let me labor,
On the mountain let me tell.'

When she sung that, it all came to me—what I was—what I was sent into the world to do—what was the cause of your loving me and bringing me out here—I saw a plan in it all. Then, too, it came to me that you would at first not see the calling as I do, but that you would say *nevertheless*, and help me, and that we would work together, and do some good in the world, you and I. Oh! I saw it all."

"Gretchen, did you see all that? Do you think that the spirit has eyes, and that they see true? But how could I begin? The Injuns all hate me."

"Make them love you."

"How?"

"Say *nevertheless* to them."

"Well, Gretchen, you are a good girl, and I am sorry for the hard things that I have said. I do not feel that I have shown just the right spirit toward Benjamin. But he has said that he will not do me any harm, for the sake of his master, and I am willin' to give up my will for my Master. It is those that give up their desires that have their desires in this world, and anybody who does an injury to another makes for himself a judgment-day of some sort. You may tell Benjamin that I am real sorry for bein' hard to him, and that, if he will come over and see me, I'll give him a carved pipe that husband made. Now, Gretchen, you may go, and I'll sit down and think a spell. I'll be dreadful lonely when you're gone."

Gretchen kissed her foster-mother at the door, and said:

"Your new spirit, mother, will make us both so happy in the future! We'll work together. What the master teaches me, I'll teach you."

"What—books?"

"Yes."

"O Gretchen, your heart is real good! But see here—my hair is gray. Oh, I am sorry—what a woman I might have been!"

Gretchen lay down in the lodge that night

beside the dusky wife of the old chief. The folds of the tent were open, and the cool winds came in from the Columbia, under the dim light of the moon and stars.

The *tepee*, or tent, was made of skins, and was adorned with picture-writing—Indian poetry (if so it might be called). Overhead were clusters of beautiful feathers and wings of birds. The old chief loved to tell her stories of these strange and beautiful wings. There were the wings of the condor, of the bald and the golden eagle, of the duck-hawk, pigeon-hawk, squirrel-hawk, of the sap-sucker, of the eider duck, and a Zenaider-like dove. Higher up were long wings of swans and albatrosses, heads of horned owls, and beaks of the laughing goose. Through the still air, from some dusky shallow of the river came the metallic calls of the river birds, like the trumpeting swan. The girl lay waking, happy in recalling the spirit with which her foster-mother had accepted her plan of life.

Suddenly her sensitive spirit became aware of something unusual and strange at the opening of the tent. There was a soft, light step without, a guarded footfall. Then a tall, dark shadow distinctly appeared, with a glitter of mother-of-pearl ornaments and a waving of plumes. It stood there like a ghost of a vivid fancy, for a time. Gretchen's heart beat. It was not an unusual thing for an Indian to come to the *tepee* late in the evening; but there was something mysterious and ominous in the bearing and atmosphere of this shadowy visitor. The form stepped within the opening of the tent, and a voice whispered, "Umatilla, awake!"

The old chief raised himself on his elbow with an "Ugh!"

"Come out under the moon."

The old chief arose and went out, and the two shadowy forms disappeared among a column of spruces on the musical banks of the Columbia.

Gretchen could not sleep. The two Indians returned late, and, as they parted, Gretchen heard Umatilla's deep voice say, "No!"

Her fears or instincts told her that the interview had reference to plots which were associated with the great Potlatch, now near at hand. She had heard the strange visitor say, "The moon is growing," and there was something shadowy in the very tone in which the words were spoken.

Mrs. Woods sat down in her home of bark and splints all alone after Gretchen's departure.

"She offers to teach me," she said to herself.

"I am so sorry that I was not able to teach her. I never read much, any way, until I came under the influence of the Methody. I might have taught her spiritual things—any one can have spiritual knowledge, and that is the highest of all. But I have loved my own will, and to give vent to my temper and tongue. I will change it all. There are times when I am my better self. I will only talk and decide upon what is best in life at such times as these. That would make my better nature grow. When I am out of sorts I will be silent-like. Heaven help me! it is hard to begin all these things when one's hair is turnin' gray, and I never knew any one's gray hair to turn young again."

She sat in the twilight crying over herself, and at last sang the mournful minor measures of a very quaint old hymn with a peculiar old history:

> "From whence doth this union arise
> That hatred is conquered by love?
> It fastens our souls in such ties
> As distance and time can't remove."

The October moon came up larger and larger night by night. It stood on the verge of the horizon now in the late afternoon, as if to see the resplendent setting of the sun. One wandered along the cool roads at the parting of day between the red sun in the west and the golden moon in the east, and felt in the light of the two worlds the melancholy change in the atmospheres of the year. The old volcanoes glistened, for a wintry crust was widening over their long-dead ovens. Mount Saint Helens, as the far range which led up to the relic of the ancient lava-floods that is now known by that name was called by the settlers, was wonderfully beautiful in the twilights of the sun and moon. Mount Hood was a celestial glory, and the shadows of the year softened the glimmering glories of the Columbia. The boatman's call echoed long and far, and the crack of the flint-lock gun leaped in its reverberations from hill to hill as though the air was a succession of hollow chambers. Water-fowl filled the streams and drifted through the air, and the forests seemed filled with young and beautiful animals full of happy life.

CHAPTER XIV.

THE POTLATCH.

A POTLATCH among the tribes of the Northwest means a feast at which some wealthy Indian gives away to his own people or to a friendly tribe all that he has. For this generosity he becomes a councilor or wise man, or judge, an attendant on the chief in public affairs, and is held in especial honor during the rest of his life.

To attain this honor of chief man or councilor, many an ambitious young Indian labors for years to amass wampum, blankets, and canoes. The feast at which he exchanges these for political honors is very dramatic and picturesque. It is usually held at the time of the full moon, and lasts for several days and nights. One of the principal features is the *Tamanous*, or Spirit-dance, which takes place at night amid blazing torches and deafening drums.

A chief rarely gives a Potlatch; he has no need of honors. But Umatilla desired to close his long and beneficent chieftainship with a gift-feast. He loved his people, and there seemed to him something noble in giving away all his private possessions to them, and trusting the care of his old age to their hearts. His chief men had done this, and had gained by it an influence which neither power nor riches can attain. This supreme influence over the hearts of his people he desired to possess. The gift-feast was held to be the noblest service that an Indian could render his race.

At the great Potlatch he would not only give away his private goods, but would take leave of the chieftainship which he had held for half a century. It was his cherished desire to see Benjamin made chief. His heart had gone into the young heart of the boy, and he longed to see The Light of the Eagle's Plume, sitting in his place amid the councilors of the nation and so beginning a new history of the ancient people.

The full moon of October is a night sun in the empires of the Columbia and the Puget Sea. No nights in the world can be more clear, lustrous, and splendid than those of the mellowing autumn in the valleys of Mount Saint Helens, Mount Hood, and

At the Cascades of the Columbia.

the Columbia. The moon rises over the crystal peaks and domes like a living glory, and mounts the deep sky amid the pale stars like a royal torch-bearer of the sun. The Columbia is a rolling flood of silver, and the gigantic trees of the centuries become a ghostly and shadowy splendor. There is a deep and reverent silence everywhere, save the cry of the water-fowl in the high air and the plash of the Cascades. Even the Chinook winds cease to blow, and the pine-tops to murmur.

It was such a night that the Potlatch began. On an open plateau overlooking the Columbia the old chief had caused a large platform to be built, and on this were piled all his canoes, his stores of blankets, his wampum, and his regal ornaments and implements of war. Around the plateau were high heaps of pine-boughs to be lighted during the Spirit-dance so as to roll a dark cloud of smoke under the bright light of the high moon, and cause a weird and dusky atmosphere.

The sun set; the shadows of night began to fall, but the plateau was silent. Not a human form was to be seen anywhere, not even on the river. Stars came out like lamps set in celestial windows, and sprinkled their rays on the crimson curtains of the evening.

The glaciers on Mount Hood began to kindle as with silver fires. The east seemed like a lifting gate of light. The great moon was rising.

Hark! At the first ray of the moon there are heard low, mysterious sounds everywhere. The forests are full of them — calls, like the coyote's bark, or bird-calls, or secret signals. They are human voices. They answer each other. There are thousands of voices calling and answering.

The full moon now hangs low over the forests, golden as the morning sun in the mists of the calm sea. There is a piercing cry and a roll of war-drums, and suddenly the edges of the forest are full of leaping and dancing forms. The plateau is alive as with an army. Pipes play, shells rattle, and drums roll, and the fantastic forms with grotesque motions pass and repass each other.

Up the Columbia comes a fleet of canoes like a cloud passing over the silvery ripples. The river is all alive with human forms, and airy paddles and the prows of tilting boats.

The plateau swarms. It is covered with waving blankets and dancing plumes. All is gayety and mirth.

There is another roll of drums, and then silence.

The circling blankets and plumes become motionless. The chief of the Cascades is coming, and with him is Benjamin and his young bride, and Gretchen.

The royal party mount the platform, and in honor of the event the torch-dance begins. A single torch flashes upon the air; another is lighted from it, another and another. A hundred are lighted—a thousand. They begin to dance and to whirl; the plateau is a dazzling scene of circling fire. Gretchen recalled the old *fêtes* amid the vineyards of the Rhine in her childhood.

Hither and thither the circles move—round and round. There is poetry in this fire-motion; and the great army of fire-dancers become excited under it, and prepared for the frenzy of the Spirit-dance that is to follow.

The torches go out. The moon turns the smoke into wannish clouds of white and yellow, which slowly rise, break, and disappear.

There is another roll of drums. Wild cries are heard in the forests. The "biters" are beginning their hunt.

Who are the biters? They are Indians in hides of bears and wolves, who run on their hands and feet, uttering terrible cries, and are followed by women, who, to make the scene more fearful, pretend to hold them back, and restrain them from violence. The Spirit-dance is held to be a sacred frenzy, and before it begins the biters are charged to hunt the woods for any who have not joined the army of dancers, and, if such are found, to bite them and tear their flesh with their teeth. They also guard the dance like sentinels, and fly at one who attempts to leave it before it is done.

The frenzied shrieks of these human animals, and of the women who follow them, produce a wonderful nervous effect upon the listening multitudes. All feel that they are about to enter into the ecstatic spiritual condition of departed souls, and are to be joined by the shades of the dead heroes and warriors of tradition and story.

Each dancer has a masque. It may be an owl's head with mother-of-pearl eyes, or a wooden pelican's beak, or a wolf's head. It may be a wooden animal's face, which can be pulled apart by a string, and reveal under it an effigy of a human face, the first masque changing into great ears. The museum at Ottawa, Canada, contains a great number of such masques, and some missionaries in the Northwest make curious collections of them.

The whirling begins. Everywhere are whirling circles—round and round they go. The sight of it all would make a spectator dizzy. Cries arise, each more and more fearful; the whole multitude are at last shrieking with dizzy heads and wildly beating pulses. The cries become deafening; an almost superhuman frenzy passes over all; they seem to be no longer mortal—the armies of the dead are believed to be about them; they think that they are reveling in the joys of the heroes' paradise. One by one they drop down, until the whole assembly is exhausted.

At midnight the great fires are kindled, and throw their lights and shadows over the frenzied sleepers. Such was the *Tamanous*-dance, and so ended the first night of the feast.

On the second night the old chief gave away his private possessions, and on the third the wedding ceremony was performed.

The wild and inhuman Death-dance, which the tribe demanded, was expected to end the festival at the going down of the shadowy moon. Could it be prevented after the traditions of unknown centuries, and at a time when the historical pride of the warriors was awakened to celebrate the barbarous deeds of their ancestors?

The wedding was simple. It consisted chiefly in gifts to the bride, Multoona. The girl was fantastically dressed, with ornaments of shells and feathers, and she followed the young prince demurely. After the ceremony of the bridal gifts came the Fire-fly dance, in which light-torches gleamed out in vanishing spirals here and there, and over all the plain. Then followed the *Tamanous* or Spirit dance, in which a peculiar kind of frenzy is excited, as has been described. The excitement was somewhat less than usual this night, on account of the great orgies which were expected to follow.

The third and great night of the Potlatch came. It was the night of the full October moon. The sun had no sooner gone down in the crimson cloud-seas among the mountains, than the moon, like another sun, broad and glorious, lifted its arch in the distant blue of the serene horizon.

The Indians gathered on the glimmering plain in the early shadows of evening, besmeared with yellow ochre and war-paint. Every head was plumed. There was a savagery in their looks that had not been seen before.

The wild dancers began their motions. The Spirit or *Tamanous* dance awakened a frenzy, and all were now impatient for the dance of the Evil Spirits to begin.

The moon hung low over the plateau and the river. The fires were kindled, and the smoke presently gave a clouded gold color to the air.

The biters were out, running hither and thither after their manner, and filling the air with hideous cries.

All was expectation, when the old chief of the Cascades stepped upon the platform, and said:

"Listen, my children—listen, O sons of the warriors of old. Twice four times sixty seasons, according to the notch-sticks, have the wings of wild geese cleaved the sky, and all these years I have lived in peace. My last moon has arisen—I have seen the smile of the Great Spirit, and I know that the last moon hangs over my head.

"Warriors, listen! You have always obeyed me. Obey me once more. Dance not the dance of the Evil Spirits to-night. Let me die in peace. Let not blood stain my last days. I want you to remember the days of Umatilla as the days of corn and maize and the pipes of peace. I have given you all I have—my days are done. You will respect me."

There were mutterings everywhere, suppressed cries of rage, and sharp words of chagrin and disappointment. The old chief saw the general dissatisfaction, and felt it like a crushing weight upon his soul.

"I am going to light the pipe of peace," said he, "and smoke it now before you. As many of you as love Umatilla, light the pipes of peace."

Not a light glimmered in the smoky air. There were words of hate and suppressed cries everywhere. A circle was forming, it widened, and it seemed as though the dreaded dance was about to begin in spite of the command of the old chief.

Suddenly a form in white stood beside Umatilla. It was Gretchen. A white arm was raised, and the martial strain of the "Wild Hunt of Lutzow" marched out like invisible horsemen, and caused every Indian to listen. Then there were a few sharp, discordant strains, and then the *Traumerei* lifted its spirit-wings of music on the air.

THE POTLATCH.

Träumerei.

BY ROBERT SCHUMANN, SIMPLIFIED BY F. BRANDEIS.
Published by permission.

Copyright, 1887, by R. A. Saalfield.

192 THE LOG SCHOOL-HOUSE ON THE COLUMBIA.

THE POTLATCH.

The murmurs ceased. The plain grew still. "Romance" followed, and then the haunting strain of the *Traumerei* rose again. It ceased. Lights began to glimmer here and there. Peace-pipes were being lighted.

"You have saved your people," said Umatilla. "Play it again."

Again and again the dream-music drifted out on the air. The plain was now filled with peace-pipes. When the last blended tones died away, the whole tribe were seated on the long plateau, and every old warrior was smoking a pipe of peace.

Gretchen saw that her spirit, through the violin, had calmed the sea. She was sure now that she had rightly read her mission in life. Amid the scene of glimmering peace-pipes, a heavenly presence seemed near her. She had broken the traditions of centuries by the sympathetic thrill of four simple strings. She felt that Von Weber was there in spirit, and Schumann. She felt that her father's soul was near her; but, more than all, she felt that she was doing the work of the Great Commission. She bowed her head on the instrument, thought of poor, terrorized Mrs. Woods in her lonely home, and wept.

A seen and unseen world had come to her—real

life. She saw her power; the gates of that mysterious kingdom, in which the reborn soul is a new creation, had been opened to her. Her spirit seemed to rise as on new-created wings, and the world to sink beneath her. She had spiritual sight, ears, and senses—a new consciousness of Divine happiness. Her purpose became strong to live for the soul alone, and she sung, over and over again, amid the silence of the peace-pipes and the rising of those puffs of smoke in the silver illumination of the high moon—

>"In the deserts let me labor,
>   On the mountains let me tell."

CHAPTER XV.

THE TRAUMEREI AGAIN.

An hour passed in this mysterious and strange tranquillity—the noon hour of night. The warriors seemed contented and satisfied. Many of them were old; some of them remembered the coming of the first ships to the Columbia, and a few of them the long visit of Vancouver. They knew the wisdom of Umatilla, and seemed proud that his will had been so readily obeyed.

But not so with the biters. They were young, and they had plotted on this night to begin hostilities against the settlers. Their plan had been to burn the log school-house and the house of the Woodses, and to make a captive of Mrs. Woods, whose hostile spirit they wished to break and punish. Soon after the quiet scene at midnight they began to be restless. Their cries arose here and there about the margin of the plateau and along the river.

THE TRAUMEREI AGAIN.

The old chief knew their feelings, and saw the stormy ripples here and there. He arose slowly, and called:

"My people, draw near."

The tribe gathered about the platform. The young braves knew what the old chief was about to say, and their cries of discontent grew loud and multiplied.

"The log school-house!" shrieked one, in a voice of rage.

"*Pil-pil!*" cried another. "*Pil-pil!*" echoed many voices. A tumult followed, and Gretchen started up from her reverie, and heard among the restless murmurs the name of Mrs. Woods.

She felt a nervous terror for a moment, but her spiritual sense and faith, which had come to her like a new-born life, returned to her.

She arose on the platform and took her violin, and looked down upon the sea of dusky faces in the smoky moonlight. She drew her bow. The music quivered. There was a lull in the excited voices. She played low, and there followed a silence.

The old chief came heavily up on the platform with a troubled face and stood beside her.

"Play the beautiful air." She played the *Traumerei* again.

The chief arose, as the last strain died away, and said:

"My people, listen."

The plateau was silent. The Columbia could be heard flowing. The trees seemed listening. Benjamin came upon the platform, reeling, and seemed about to speak to his father, but the old chief did not heed.

"My people, listen," repeated the chief.

A wild shriek of pain rent the air, and Benjamin dropped at the feet of his father. It was his voice that uttered the cry of agony and despair as he fell.

What had happened?

The boy lay on the platform as one dead. The old chief bent over him and laid his hand on his face. He started back as he did so, for the face was cold. But the boy's eyes pitifully followed every movement of his father. Gretchen sunk down beside the body, and drew her hand across his forehead and asked for water. Benjamin knew her.

Soon his voice came again. He looked wistfully toward Gretchen and said:

"I shall never go to find the Black Eagle's nest again. It is the plague. My poor father!—my poor father!"

"Send for the medicine-man," said the chief. "Quick!"

Hopping-Bear, the old medicine-man, came, a dreadful figure in eagle's plumes and bear-skins. To affect the imagination of the people when he was going to visit the sick, he had been accustomed to walk upon his two hands and one foot, with the other foot moving up and down in the air. He believed that sickness was caused by obsession, or the influence of some evil spirit, and he endeavored, by howlings, jumpings, and rattling of snake-skins, to drive this imaginary spirit away. But he did not begin his incantations here; he looked upon Benjamin with staring eyes, and cried out:

"It is the plague!"

The old chief of the Cascades lifted his helpless face to the sky.

"The stars are gone out!" he said. "I care for nothing more."

The boy at times was convulsed, then lay for a time unconscious after the convulsions, then consciousness would return. In one of these moments of consciousness he asked of Gretchen:

"Where is Boston tilicum?"

"He is not here—he does not know that you are sick."

"Run for him; tell him I can't go to the Missouri with him. I can't find the Black Eagle's nest. Run!"

His mind was dreaming and wandering.

Gretchen sent a runner to bring the schoolmaster to the dreadful scene.

A convulsion passed over the boy, but he revived again.

"Have faith in Heaven," said Gretchen. "There is One above that will save you."

"One above that will save me! Are you sure?"

"Yes," said Gretchen.

She added:

"Mother is sorry for what she said to you."

"I am sorry," said the boy, pathetically.

He was lost again in spasms of pain. When he revived, Marlowe Mann had come. The boy lifted his eyes to his beloved teacher vacantly; then the light of intelligence came back to them, and he knew him.

"I can't go," he said. "We shall never go to the lakes of the honks together. Boston tilicum, I am going to die; I am going away like my brothers —where?"

It was near the gray light of the morning, and a flock of wild geese were heard trumpeting in the air. The boy heard the sound, and started.

"Boston tilicum!"

"What can I do for you?"

"Boston tilicum, listen. Do you hear? What taught the honks where to go?"

"The Great Father of all."

"He leads them?"

"Yes."

"He will lead me?"

"Yes."

"And teach me when I am gone away. I can trust him. But my father—my father! Boston tilicum, he loves me, and he is old."

Flock after flock of wild geese flew overhead in the dim light. The boy lay and listened. He seemed to have learned a lesson of faith from the instincts of these migratory birds. He once turned to the master and said, almost in Gretchen's words:

"There is One above that will save me."

As the morning drew nearer, the air seemed filled with a long procession of Canadian geese going toward the sea. The air rang with their calls. The poor boy seemed to think that somehow they were calling to him.

There was silence at last in the air, and he turned toward Gretchen his strangely quiet face, and said, "Play."

Gretchen raised her bow. As she did so a sharp spasm came over him. He lifted his hand and tried to feel of one of the feathers from the Black Eagle's nest. He was evidently wandering to the Falls of the Missouri. His hand fell. He passed into a stertorous sleep, and lay there, watched by the old chief and the silent tribe.

Just as the light of early morn was flaming through the tall, cool, dewy trees, the breathing became labored, and ceased.

There he lay in the rising sun, silent and dead, with the helpless chief standing statue-like above him, and the tribe, motionless as a picture, circled around him, and with Gretchen at his feet.

"Make way!" said the old chief, in a deep voice.

He stepped down from the platform, and walked in a kingly manner, yet with tottering steps, toward the forest. Gretchen followed him. He heard her step, but did not look around.

"White girl, go back," he said; "I want to be alone."

He entered the forest slowly and disappeared.

Just at night he was seen coming out of the forest again. He spoke to but a single warrior, and only said:

"Bury him as the white men bury; open the blanket of the earth; and command the tribe to be there — to-morrow at sundown. Take them all away—I will watch. Where is the white girl?"

"She has gone home," said the Indian.

"Then I will watch alone. Take them all away—I want to be alone. It is the last night of the chief of the Umatillas. It is the last watch of the stars. My blood is cold, my heart beats slow—it will not be long!"

The chief sat all night by the body. In the morning he went to his lodge, and the tribe made the preparations for the funeral, and opened a grave in the earth.

CHAPTER XVI.

A SILENT TRIBE.

It was sunset on the bluffs and valleys of the Columbia. Through the tall, dark pines and firs the red west glowed like the lights in an oriel or mullioned window. The air was voiceless. The Columbia rolled silently in the shadows with a shimmering of crimson on its deep middle tides. The long, brown boats of the salmon-fishers sat motionless on the tide. Among the craft of the fishermen glided a long, airy canoe, with swift paddles. It contained an old Umatilla Indian, his daughter, and a young warrior. The party were going to the young chief's funeral.

As the canoe glided on amid the still fishermen of other tribes, the Indian maiden began to sing. It was a strange song, of immortality, and of spiritual horizons beyond the visible life. The Umatillas have poetic minds. To them white

Multnomah Falls.

Tacoma with her gushing streams means a mother's breast, and the streams themselves, like the Falls of the distant Shoshone, were "falling splendors."

She sang in Chinook, and the burden of her song was that horizons will lift forever in the unknown future. The Chinook word *tamala* means "to-morrow"; and to-morrow, to the Indian mind, was eternal life.

The young warrior joined in the refrain, and the old Indian listened. The thought of the song was something as follows:

"Aha! it is ever to-morrow, to-morrow—
   Tamala, tamala, sing as we row;
Lift thine eye to the mount; to the wave give thy sorrow;
   The river is bright, and the rivulets flow;
     Tamala, tamala,
     Ever and ever;
The morrows will come and the morrows will go—
        Tamala! tamala!

"Happy boat, it is ever to-morrow, to-morrow—
   Tamala, whisper the waves as they flow;
The crags of the sunset the smiles of light borrow,
   And soft from the ocean the Chinook winds blow:
     Tamala, tamala,
     Ever and ever;
The morrows will come and the morrows will go—
        Tamala! tamala!

"Aha! the night comes, but the light is to-morrow—
   Tamala, tamala, sing as we go;

> The waves ripple past, like the heart-beats of sorrow,
>   And the oar beats the wave to our song as we row:
>   Tamala, tamala,
>   Ever and ever;
> The morrows will come and the morrows will go—
>   Tamala! tamala!
>
> "For ever and ever horizons are lifting—
>   Tamala, tamala, sing as we row;
> And life toward the stars of the ocean is drifting,
>   Through death will the morrow all endlessly glow—
>   Tamala, tamala,
>   Ever and ever;
> The morrows will come and the morrows will go,
>   Tamala! tamala!"

The paddle dipped in the wave at the word *tamala*, and lifted high to mark the measure of the song, and strew in the warm, soft air the watery jewels colored by the far fires of the Sound. So the boat swept on, like a spirit bark, and the beautiful word of immortality was echoed from the darkening bluffs and the primitive pine cathedrals.

The place where the grave had been made was on the borders of the Oregon desert, a wild, open region, walled with tremendous forests, and spreading out in the red sunset like a sea. It had a scanty vegetation, but a slight rain would sometimes change it into a billowy plain of flowers.

The tribe had begun to assemble about the grave early in the long afternoon. They came one by one, solitary and silent, wrapped in blankets and ornamented with gray plumes. The warriors came in the same solitary way and met in silence, and stood in a long row like an army of shadows. Squaws came, leading children by the hand, and seated themselves on the soft earth in the same stoical silence that had marked the bearing of the braves.

A circle of lofty firs, some three hundred feet high, threw a slanting shadow over the open grave, the tops gleaming with sunset fire.

Afar, Mount Hood, the dead volcano, lifted its roof of glaciers twelve thousand feet high. Silver ice and black carbon it was now, although in the long ages gone it had had a history written in flame and smoke and thunder. Tradition says that it sometimes, even now, rumbles and flashes forth in the darkness of night, then sinks into rest again, under its lonely ice palaces so splendid in the sunset, so weird under the moon.

Just as the red disk of the sun sunk down behind this stupendous scenery, a low, guttural sound was uttered by Potlatch Hero, an old Indian brave, and it passed along the line of the shadowy braves. No one moved, but all eyes were turned toward the lodge of the old Umatilla chief.

He was coming—slowly, with measured step; naked, except the decent covering of a blanket and a heroic ornament of eagle-plumes, and all alone.

The whole tribe had now gathered, and a thousand dusky forms awaited him in the sunset.

There was another guttural sound. Another remarkable life-picture came into view. It was the school in a silent procession, following the tall masks, out of the forest trail on to the glimmering plain, the advent of that new civilization before which the forest lords, once the poetic bands of the old Umatillas, were to disappear. Over all a solitary eagle beat the luminous air, and flocks of wild geese made their way, like V-letters, toward the Puget Sea.

The school soon joined the dusky company, and the pupils stood with uncovered heads around their Yankee-pedagogue. But the old chief came slowly. After each few steps he would stop, fold his arms, and seem lost in contemplation. These pauses were longer as he drew near the silent company.

Except the honks of the pilots of the flocks of wild geese, there was a dead silence everywhere. Only eyes moved, and then furtively, toward the advancing chief.

He reached the grave at last by these slow movements, and stepped upon the earth that had

The old chief stood stoical and silent.

been thrown out of it, and folded his arms in view of all. A golden star, like a lamp in the windows of heaven, hung over Mount Hood in the fading splendors of the twilight, and the great chief bent his eye upon it.

Suddenly the air was rent by a wail, and a rattle of shells and drums. The body of Benjamin was being brought out of the lodge. It was borne on a bier made of poles, and covered with boughs of pine and fir and red mountain phlox. It was wrapped in a blanket, and strewn with odorous ferns. Four young braves bore it, besmeared with war-paint. They were followed by musicians, who beat their drums, and rattled shell instruments at irregular times, as they advanced. They came to the grave, lifted the body on its blanket from the bier of evergreens and flowers, and slowly lowered it. The old chief stood stoical and silent, his eye fixed on the star in the darkening shadows.

The face of Benjamin was noble and beautiful in its death-sleep. Over it were two black eagle's plumes. The deep black hair lay loosely about the high, bronze forehead; there was an expression of benevolence in the compressed lips, and the helpless hands seemed like a picture as they lay crossed on each other.

been thrown out of it, and folded his arms in view of all. A golden star, like a lamp in the windows of heaven, hung over Mount Hood in the fading splendors of the twilight, and the great chief bent his eye upon it.

Suddenly the air was rent by a wail, and a rattle of shells and drums. The body of Benjamin was being brought out of the lodge. It was borne on a bier made of poles, and covered with boughs of pine and fir and red mountain phlox. It was wrapped in a blanket, and strewn with odorous ferns. Four young braves bore it, besmeared with war-paint. They were followed by musicians, who beat their drums, and rattled shell instruments at irregular times, as they advanced. They came to the grave, lifted the body on its blanket from the bier of evergreens and flowers, and slowly lowered it. The old chief stood stoical and silent, his eye fixed on the star in the darkening shadows.

The face of Benjamin was noble and beautiful in its death-sleep. Over it were two black eagle's plumes. The deep black hair lay loosely about the high, bronze forehead; there was an expression of benevolence in the compressed lips, and the helpless hands seemed like a picture as they lay crossed on each other.

As soon as the body was laid in the earth, the old chief bent his face on the people. The mysterious dimness of death was in his features. His eyes gleamed, and his bronze lips were turning pale.

"My nation, listen; 'tis my last voice. I am a Umatilla. In my youth the birds in the free lakes of the air were not more free. I spoke, and you obeyed. I have but one more command to give. Will you obey me?

"You bow, and I am glad.

"Listen!

"My fathers were men of war. They rolled the battle-drums. I taught my warriors to play the pipes of peace, and sixty years have they played them under the great moons of the maize-fields. We were happy. I was happy.

"I had seven sons. The white man's plague came; the shadow fell on six of them, and they went away with the storm-birds. They entered the new canoe, and sailed beyond us on the sea of life. They came back no more at the sunrisings and sun settings, at the leaf-gatherings of the spring, or the leaf-fallings of the autumn. They are beyond.

"One son was left me—Benjamin. He was no

common youth; the high spirits were with him, and he came to be like them, and he has gone to them now. I loved him. He was my eyes; he was my ears; he was my heart. When I saw his eyes in death, my eyes were dead; when he could hear me call his name no longer, my ears lost their hearing; when his young heart ceased to beat, my own heart was dead. All that I am lies in that grave, beside my dead boy.

"My nation, you have always obeyed me. I have but one more command to make. Will you obey me?

"You bow again. My life-blood is growing cold. I am about to go down into that grave.

"One step! The clouds fly and darken, and you will see them return again, but not I.

"Two steps! Farewell, sun and light of day. I shall see thee again, but not as now.

"Three steps! Downward to the grave I descend to meet thee, my own dear boy. Adieu, my people. Adieu, hearts of faith. Farewell, ye birds of the air, ye mighty forests, ye sun of night, and ye marches of stars. I am dying.

"Two steps more I will take. There he lies before me in the unfolded earth, the life of my life, the heart of my heart.

"You have promised to obey me. I repeat it—you have promised to obey me. You have always done so. You must do so now. My hands are cold, my feet are cold, and my heart beats very slow. Three steps more, and I shall lay myself on the body of my boy. Hear, then, my last command; you have promised to obey it like brave men.

"When I have taken my last three steps of life, and laid down beside the uncovered bed of earth beside my boy, fill up the grave forever; my breath will be gone; Umatilla will be no more. You must obey.

"One step—look! There is fire on the mountain under the curtains of the night. Look, the peak flashes; it is on fire.—O Spirit of All, I come! One step more! Farewell, earth. Warriors, fill the grave! The black eagle's plumes will now rest forever."

There was deep silence, broken only by the sobs of the little school. A warrior moved and passed round the grave, and uttered the word "Dead!" The braves followed him, and the whole tribe like shadows. "Dead!" "Dead!" passed from mouth to mouth. Then a warrior threw a handful of earth into the grave of the father and son. The braves followed his example, then all the tribe.

As they were so doing, like phantoms in the dim light, Mount Saint Helens* blazed again—one volcanic flash, then another; then all was darkness, and the moon arose in a broad sea of light like a spectral sun.

The grave was filled at last. Then they brought the Cayuse pony of Benjamin toward the grave, and a young brave raised the hatchet to kill it, that it might bear the dead boy into the unknown land.

There was a cry! It came from Gretchen. The girl rushed forward and stood before the hatchet. The pony seemed to know her, and he put his head over her shoulder.

"Spare him!" she said. "Benjamin gave him to me—the soul of Benjamin would wish it so."

"Let the girl have her way," said the old warriors.

The moon now moved free in the dark-blue sky, and sky, forest, and plain were a silver sea. The Indians began to move away like shadows, one by one, silent and slow. Gretchen was the last to go. She followed the school, leading the pony, her soul filled with that consciousness of a new life that had so wonderfully come to her. Her way in

---

* See Notes.

life now seemed clear: she must teach the Umatillas.

She left the pony in a grassy clearing, on the trail that led to her home, and hurried toward the cabin to describe all the events of the day to her foster-mother.

CHAPTER XVII.

A DESOLATE HOME AND A DESOLATE PEOPLE.

As Gretchen was hurrying home on the evening after these exciting scenes, she met Mrs. Woods in the trail, and she saw at a glance that her foster-mother was in great distress.

"O Gretchen," she said, "I am so glad that you have come—you are all that is left to me now! I am all alone in the world! Have you heard it, Gretchen?"

"What, mother?"

"Husband is drowned!"

Mrs. Woods seized the arm of the girl, and the two helpless women hurried toward their rude home, each to relate to the other a scene of distress, and each to wonder what the wide future had in store for them.

They held each other by the hand, and talked in the open door of the cabin. Then they went in and ate a simple meal of milk and berries, and lay down and slept the sleep of sorrow.

At the early light they awoke. Almost the first words that Gretchen spoke were: "Let us face life and be fearless. I have faith. My father had faith, and my mother lived by faith. It was faith that led them across the sea. Their faith seemed to be unfulfilled, but it will be fulfilled in me. I feel it. Mother, let trouble pass. We belong to the family of God."

"You are a comfort to me, Gretchen. I can not see my way—it is covered."

"But you can trust your Guide, mother, and the end of trust is peace."

"What are we to do, Gretchen?"

"I will go to Walla Walla and seek the advice of Mrs. Spaulding."

"Gretchen, don't you think that the schoolmaster is a good man?"

"Yes, I am sure that he is."

"I am. Let us go to him and follow his advice. We will go together."

They agreed to make the visit on the following day in the morning, before school.

Gretchen told her foster-mother the story of the Indian pony.

"Where is he now?" asked Mrs. Woods.

"I left him in the clearing. I will go and find him."

"I will go with you," said Mrs. Woods.

The two went out together. They came to the clearing—a place of waving grass, surrounded with gigantic trees, in whose tops were great nests of birds. The pony was not there.

"He has gone to the next clearing," said Gretchen.

They passed through a strip of wood to another clearing. But the pony was not there.

As they were returning, a little black animal crossed their path.

Mrs. Woods said, "Hold!" then called out in a kindly voice, "Roll over." The little animal rolled head over heels in a very comical way, then ran quickly into the thick bushes. It was the last time that Mrs. Woods ever saw little Roll Over, and Gretchen never saw the pony again. The latter probably found a herd of horses and wandered away with them. It was a time of such confusion and distress that the matter did not awaken the interest of the Indians at that time.

That evening they talked of plans for the future.

"Let us seek work in one of the missionary stations," said Gretchen, "or let us find a home among the Indians themselves. I want to become a teacher among them, and I know that they would treat you well."

Mrs. Woods's views on these matters were changing, but something of her old distrust and prejudice remained despite her good resolutions.

"Foxes and geese were never made to hold conference meetings together. You can't make one man out of another if you try."

"But, mother, your English ancestors once wandered about in sheep-skins, and worshiped the oaks; the whole English race, and the German race, were made what they are by teachers — teachers who gave themselves to a cause almost two thousand years ago."

"Yes, I suppose that is so. But, Gretchen, I want your heart; I never thought that you would give it to the Injuns. I ought not to be so ruled by my affections; but, if I do scold you, there is something in you that draws my heart toward you all the time. I believe in helping others; something good in the future always comes of it. If men would be good to each other, Heaven would be good to the world. It is the things done here in this world that are out of order, and I never was on very good terms with myself even, not to say much of the world. But you have helped me, Gretchen, and hymns have helped me. I want you to be charitable toward my feelins', Gretchen, when I grow old, and I pray that you will always be true to me."

"I shall always be true to you, whatever I may be called to do. I shall not leave you until you give your consent. One day you will wish me to do as I have planned—I feel it within me; something is leading me, and our hearts will soon be one in my plan of life."

"It may be so, Gretchen. I have had a hard time, goin' out to service when I was a girl. My only happy days were during the old Methody preaching of Jason Lee. I thought I owned the heavens then. It was then I married, and I said to husband: 'Here we must always be slaves, and life will be master of us; let us go West, and own a free farm, and be masters of life.' There is a great deal in being master of life. Well, we have had a hard time, but husband has been good to me, and you have made me happy, if I have scolded. Gretchen, some people kiss each other by scoldin'; I do—I scold to make the world better. I suppose everything is for the best, after all. There is no experience in life that does not teach us something, and there is a better world beyond that awaits all who desire a better life. Our desires are better than ourselves—mine are. Good desires are prayers, and I think that they will all be answered some day."

She sat in silence, thinking of her lonely situation, of her ignorance and imperfection, of her often baffled struggles to do well in this world and to overcome her poor, weak self, and she burst into tears.

"Play," she said. "Music is a kind of prayer." And Gretchen touched the musical glasses.

CHAPTER XVIII.

THE LIFTED CLOUD—THE INDIANS COME TO THE SCHOOLMASTER.

THE next day witnessed a strange scene at the log school-house on the Columbia. It was a red October morning. Mrs. Woods accompanied Gretchen to the school, as she wished to have a talk with Mr. Mann.

As the two came in sight of the house, Mrs. Woods caught Gretchen by the arm and said:

"What's *them?*"

"Where?"

"Sittin' in the school-yard."

"They are Indians."

"Injuns? What are they there for?"

"I don't know, mother."

"Come for advice, like me, may be."

"Perhaps they are come to school. The old chief told them that I would teach them."

"You?"

"They have no father now."

"No father?"

"No chief."

Mrs. Woods had been so overwhelmed with her own grief that she had given little thought to the death of Benjamin and the chief of the Cascades. The unhappy condition of the little tribe now came to her as in a picture; and, as she saw before her some fifty Indians seated on the ground, her good heart came back to her, and she said, touched by a sense of her own widowhood, "Gretchen, I pity 'em."

Mrs. Woods was right. These Indians had come to seek the advice of Mr. Mann in regard to their tribal affairs. Gretchen also was right. They had come to ask Mr. Mann to teach their nation.

It was an unexpected assembly that Marlowe Mann faced as he came down the clearing, but it revealed to him, at a glance, his future work in life.

The first of the distressed people to meet him was Mrs. Woods.

"O Mr. Mann, I am all alone in the world, and what am I goin' to do? There's nothin' but hard days' work left to me now, and—hymns. Even Father Lee has gone, and I have no one to advise me. You will be a friend to me, won't you?"

"Yes," said Mr. Mann. "I need you, and the way is clear."

"What do you mean?"

"I have a letter from Boston."

"What is it, Marlowe Mann?"

"The Indian Educational Society have promised me a thousand dollars for my work another year. I must have a house. I would want you to take charge of it. *But*—your tongue?"

"O Master Mann, I'll give up my tongue! I'll just work, and be still. If an Injun will give up his revenge, an' it's his natur', ought not I to give up my tongue? When I can't help scoldin' I'll just sing hymns."

Mr. Mann gazed into the faces of the Indians. The warm sunlight fell upon them. There was a long silence, broken only by the scream of the eagles in the sky and the passing of flocks of wild geese. Then one of the Indians rose and said:

"Umatilla has gone to his fathers.

"Benjamin has gone to his fathers. We shall never see Young Eagle's plume again!

"Bostom tilicum, be our chief. We have come to school."

Mr. Mann turned to Gretchen. Her young

face was lovely that morning with sympathy. He said in a low voice:

"You see *our* work in life. Do you understand? Will you accept it?"

She understood his heart.

"I will do whatever you say."

In 1859 a great Indian Reservation was established in what is known in Oregon as the Inland Empire of the Northwest. It contained about two hundred and seventy thousand acres, agricultural land and timber-land. The beautiful Umatilla River flows through it. The agency now is near Pendleton, Oregon. Thither the Umatillas were removed.

Marlowe Mann went there, and Gretchen as his young wife, and in their home Mrs. Woods for many years could have been heard singing hymns.

Their home stood for the Indian race, and the schoolmaster and his wife devoted themselves to the cause of Indian education. Through the silent influence of Mr. Mann's correspondence with the East, Indian civilization was promoted, and the way prepared for the peaceful settlement of the great Northwest.

Gretchen taught the Indians as long as she lived. Often at evening, when the day's work had been hard, she would take her violin, and a dream of music would float upon the air. She played but one tune at last as she grew serenely old. That tune recalled her early German home, the Rhine, her good father and mother, and the scenes of the great Indian Potlatch on the Columbia. It was the *Traumerei*.

Her poetic imagination, which had been suppressed by her foster-mother in her girlhood, came back to her in her new home, and it was her delight to express in verse the inspirations of her life amid these new scenes, and to publish these poems in the papers of the East that most sympathized with the cause of Indian education.

The memory of Benjamin and the old chief of the Cascades never left her. It was a never-to-be-forgotten lesson of the nobility of all men whose souls have the birthright of heaven. Often, when the wild geese were flying overhead in the evening, she would recall Benjamin, and say, "He who guides led me here from the Rhine, and schooled me for my work in the log school-house on the Columbia."

Such is not an overdrawn picture of the early pioneers of the Columbia and the great Northwest.

Jason Lee was censured for leaving his mission for the sake of Oregon—for turning his face from the stars to the sun. Whitman, when he appeared ragged at Washington, was blamed for having left his post. The early pioneers of the great Northwest civilization lie in neglected graves. We are now beginning to see the hand of Providence, and to realize how great was the work that these people did for their own country and for the world.

And Marlowe Mann—whose name stands for the Christian schoolmaster—no one knows where he sleeps now; perhaps no one, surely but a few. He saw his college-mates rise to honor and fame. They offered him positions, but he knew his place in the world.

When his hair was turning gray, there came to him an offer of an opportunity for wealth, from his remaining relatives. At the same time the agency offered him the use of a farm. He accepted the latter for his work's sake, and returned to his old friends a loving letter and an old poem, and with the latter we will leave this picture of old times on the Oregon:

"Happy the man whose wish and care
    A few paternal acres bound;
Content to breathe his native air
    On his own ground.

"Whose herds with milk, whose fields with bread,
    Whose flocks supply him with attire;
Whose trees in summer yield him shade,
    In winter, fire.

"Sound sleep by night, study and ease,
    Together mixed sweet recreation:
And innocence, which most doth please,
    With meditation.

"Blessed who can unconcernedly find
    Hours, days, and years glide soft away,
In health of body, peace of mind;
    Quiet by day.

"Thus let me live unseen, unknown;
    Thus unlamented let me die;
Steal from the world, and not a stone
    Tell where I lie."

HISTORICAL NOTES.

I.

VANCOUVER.

The remarkable progress of the Pacific port cities of Seattle and Tacoma make Washington an especially bright, new star on the national flag. Surrounded as these cities are with some of the grandest and most poetic scenery in the United States, with gigantic forests and rich farm-lands, with mountains of ores, with coal-mines, iron-mines, copper-mines, and mines of the more precious treasures; washed as they are by the water of noble harbors, and smiled upon by skies of almost continuous April weather—there must be a great future before the cities of Puget Sound.

The State of Washington is one of the youngest in the Union, and yet she is not too young to celebrate soon the one-hundredth anniversary of several interesting events.

It was on the 15th of December, 1790, that Captain George Vancouver received his commission as commander of his Majesty's sloop of war the Discovery. Three of his officers were Peter Puget, Joseph Baker, and Joseph Whidby, whose names now live in Puget Sound—Mount Baker, and Whidby Island.

The great island of British Columbia, and its energetic port city, received the name of Vancouver himself, and Vancouver named most of the places on Puget Sound in honor of his personal friends. He must have had a heart formed for friendship, thus to have immortalized those whom he esteemed and loved. It is the discovery and the naming of mountains, islands, and ports of the Puget Sound that suggest poetic and patriotic celebrations.

The old journals of Vancouver lie before us. In these we read:

"From this direction, round by the north and northwest, the high, distant land formed, like detached islands, among which the lofty mountains discovered in the afternoon by the third lieutenant, and in compliment to him called by me Mount Baker, rose to a very conspicuous object."

It was on Monday, April 30, 1792, that Mount

Baker was thus discovered and named. In May, 1792, Vancouver states that he came to a "very safe" and "capatious" harbor, and that "to this port I gave the name of Port Townshend, in honor of the noble marquis of that name."

Again, on Thursday, May 29, 1792, Vancouver discovered another excellent port, and says:

"This harbor, after the gentleman who discovered it, obtained the name of Port Orchard."

In May, 1792, he makes the following very important historical note:

"Thus by our joint efforts we had completely explored every turning of this extensive inlet; and, to commemorate Mr. Puget's exertions, the fourth extremity of it I named Puget Sound."

A very interesting officer seems to have been this lieutenant, Peter Puget, whose soundings gave the name to the American Mediterranean. Once, after the firing of muskets to overawe hostile Indians, who merely pouted out their lips, and uttered, "Poo hoo! poo hoo!" he ordered the discharge of a heavy gun, and was amused to note the silence that followed. It was in April and May, 1792, that Puget explored the violet waters of the great inland sea, a work which he seems to have done with the enthusiasm of a romancer as well as of a naval officer.

Mount Hood was named for Lord Hood, and Mount Saint Helens was named in 1792, in the month of October, "in honor of his Britannic Majesty's ambassador at the court of Madrid." But one of the most interesting of all of Vancouver's notes is the following:

"The weather was serene and pleasant, and the country continued to exhibit the same luxuriant appearance. At its northern extremity Mount Baker bore compass; the round, snowy mountain, now forming its southern extremity, after my friend Rear-Admiral Ranier, I distinguished by the name of Mount Ranier. May, 1792." This mountain is now Mount Tacoma.

The spring of 1892 ought to be historically very interesting to the State of Washington, and it is likely to be so.

II.

THE OREGON TRAIL.

"There is the East. There lies the road to India."

Such was Senator Thomas H. Benton's view of the coast and harbors of Oregon. He saw the advantage of securing to the United States the Columbia River and its great basin, and the Puget Sea; and he made himself the champion of Oregon and Washington.

In Thomas Jefferson's administration far-seeing people began to talk of a road across the continent, and a port on the Pacific. The St. Louis fur-traders had been making a way to the Rockies for years, and in 1810 John Jacob Astor sent a ship around Cape Horn, to establish a post for the fur-trade on the Pacific Coast, and also sent an expedition of some sixty persons from St. Louis, overland, by the way of the Missouri and Yellowstone, to the Columbia River. The pioneer ship was called the Tonquin. She arrived at the mouth of the Columbia before the overland expedition. These traders came together at last, and founded Astoria, on the Columbia.

Ships now began to sail for Astoria, and the trading-post flourished in the beautiful climate and amid the majestic scenery. But the English claimed the country. In June, 1812, war broke out with England, and Astoria became threatened with capture by the English. It was decided by Astor's agent to abandon the post; but Astoria had taught the United States the value of Oregon.

The Oregon trail from St. Louis, by the way of

the great rivers, the Missouri, the Yellowstone, and the Columbia, followed the fall of Astoria, and began the highway of emigration to the Pacific coast and to Asia. Over it the trapper and the missionary began to go. The Methodist missionaries, under the leadership of Revs. Jason and Daniel Lee, were among the first in the field, and laid the foundations of the early cities of Oregon. One of their stations was at the Dalles of the Columbia. In 1835 the great missionary, Marcus Whitman, of the Congregationalist Board, established the mission at Walla Walla. Yet up to the year 1841, just fifty years ago, only about one hundred and fifty Americans, in all, had permanently settled in Oregon and Washington.

Senator Benton desired the survey of a route to Oregon, to aid emigration to the Columbia basin. He engaged for this service a young, handsome, gallant, and chivalrous officer, Lieutenant John C. Fremont, who, with Nicollet, a French naturalist, had been surveying the upper Mississippi, and opening emigration to Minnesota.

Fremont espoused not only the cause of Oregon, but also Senator Benton's young daughter Jessie, who later rendered great personal services to her husband's expedition in the Northwest.

Kit Carson was the guide of this famous expedition. The South Pass was explored, and the flag planted on what is now known as Fremont's Peak, and the country was found to be not the Great American Desert of the maps, but a land of wonderful beauty and fertility. In 1843 Fremont made a second expedition; this time from the South Pass to the Columbia country. After he was well on his way, the War Department recalled him; but Mrs. Fremont suppressed the order, in the interest of the expedition, until it was too late to reach him.

Fremont went by the way of Salt Lake, struck the Oregon trail, and finally came to the mission that Dr. Whitman had founded among the Nez-Percés (pierced noses) at Walla Walla. This mission then consisted of a single adobe house.

The British claimants of the territory, finding that American immigration was increasing, began to bring settlers from the Red River of the North. A struggle now began to determine which country should possess this vast and most important territory. When Dr. Whitman learned of the new efforts of the English to settle the country, and the danger of losing Oregon by treaties pending at Washington, he started for St. Louis, by the way of Santa Fé. This ride, often called "Whitman's Ride for Oregon," is one of the poetical events of American history. He went to Washington, was treated cavalierly by the State Department, but secured a delay of the treaties, which proved the means of saving Oregon and Washington to the United States.

So his missionary efforts gave to our country an empire that seems destined to become ultimate America, and a power in the Asian world.

III.

GOVERNOR STEVENS.

In the long line of brave American soldiers, General Isaac Ingalls Stevens deserves a noble rank in the march of history. He was born at Andover, Mass., and was educated at West Point, where he was graduated from the Military Academy in 1839 with the highest honors. He was on the military staff of General Scott in Mexico, and held other honorable positions in the Government service in his early life.

But the great period of his life was his survey

of the Northern route to the Pacific, since largely followed by the Northern Pacific Railroad, and his development of Washington Territory as a pioneer Governor. He saw the road to China by the way of the Puget Sea, and realized that Washington stood for the East of the Eastern Continent and the Western. He seems to have felt that here the flag would achieve her greatest destiny, and he entered upon his work like a knight who faced the future and not the past. His survey of the Northern Pacific route led the march of steam to the Puget Sea, and the great steamers have carried it forward to Japan, China, and India.

His first message to the Legislature at Olympia (1854) was a map of the future and a prophecy. It was a call for roads, schools, a university, and immigration. The seal of Washington was made to bear the Indian word *Alké*—"by and by"—or "in the future." It also was a prophecy.

He created the counties of Sawanish, Whatcom, Clallam, Chehalis, Cowlitz, Wahkiakum, Skamania, and Walla Walla. Olympia was fixed upon as the seat of government, and measures were taken by the Government for the regulation of the Indian tribes.

Stevens was the military leader of the Indian

war. He reduced the tribes to submission, and secured a permanent peace. He was elected to Congress as a Territorial delegate in 1857, and sought at Washington as earnestly as on the Puget Sea the interests of the rising State.

He was a man of great intellect, of a forceful and magnetic presence—a man born to lead in great emergencies. He carried New England ideas and traditions to the Pacific, and established them there for all time to come, creating there a greater New England which should gather to its harbors the commerce of the world.

Governor Stevens was a conservative in politics, but when the news of the fall of Sumter thrilled the country, he said to the people of Olympia, "I conceive it my duty to stop disunion." He went to Washington and entered the Union service.

He fell like a hero at Chantilly, and under the flag which he had taken from his color-bearer, who had received a mortal wound. His was a splendid career that the nation should honor. We recently saw his sword and historic pictures at the home of his widow and son at Dorchester, Mass., and were impressed with these relics of a spirit that had done so much for the progress of the country and mankind.

The State of Washington is his monument, and progressive thought his eulogy. His great mind and energy brought order out of chaos, and set the flag in whose folds he died forever under the gleaming dome of the Colossus of American mountains and over the celestial blue of the Pacific harbors of the Puget Sea.

IV.

SEATTLE THE CHIEF.

Seattle was a Dwamish chief, and a true friend of the white race, whom he seemed to follow on account of their superior intelligence. He gave the name to an early settlement, which is now a great city, and which seems destined to become one of the important port cities of the world; for when in 1852, some forty years ago, the pioneers of Alké Point left the town which they had laid out and called New York, and removed to the other side of the bay, they named the place Seattle, from the friendly chief, instead of New York. Alké means *by and by*, and Seattle is likely to become the New York of the Pacific, and one of the great ports for Asiatic trade. With the immense agricultural and mineral resources with which it is surrounded, with its inexhaustible stores of timber, its sublime scenery and delightful climate, with its direct and natural water-road to Japan and China, and its opportunity of manufacturing for the Asiatic market the kind of goods that England has to carry to the same markets over an adventurous course of three times the distance, with the great demand for grain among the rice-eating countries of the East—the mind can not map the possibilities of this port city for the next hundred years or more. The prophecy of its enterprising citizens, that it will one day be one of the great cities in the world, is not unlikely to be realized; and it is interesting to ask what was the history of the chief who gave the name to this new Troy of the Puget Sea.

He was at this time somewhat advanced in life, a portly man, of benevolent face, recalling the picture of Senator Benton, of Missouri, whom he was said to resemble. He was the chief of the Dwamishes, a small tribe inhabiting the territory around what is now Elliott Bay. He became a friend of Dr. Maynard, one of the pioneers of the new town, and of General Stevens, the great Territorial Governor. He was well known to Foster, Denny, Bell, and Borden, who took claims where the city now stands. His last years were passed at Port Madison, where he died in 1866, at a great age.

Governor Stevens confirmed his sachemship, and Seattle became the protector and the good genius of the town. A curious legend, which seems to be well founded, is related of a tax which Seattle levied upon the new town, for the sake of the trouble that the name would give him in the spiritual world. When a Dwamish Indian lost a near relative of the same name by death, he changed his own name, because the name might attract the ghost of the deceased, and so cause him to be haunted. The tribe believed that departed spirits loved their old habitations, and the associations of their names and deeds, and so they changed their names and places on the death of relatives, that they might not be disturbed by ghostly apparitions.

"Why do you ask for a tax?" asked a pioneer of Seattle.

"The name of the town will call me back after I am dead, and make me unhappy. I want my pay for what I shall suffer then, now."

I hope that the rapid growth of the great city of the North does not disquiet the gentle and benevolent soul of Seattle. The city should raise a monument to him, that he may see that he is kindly remembered when he comes back to visit the associations of his name and life. Or, better for his shade, the city should kindly care for his daughter, poor old Angeline Seattle, who at the time of this writing (1890) is a beggar in the streets of uplifting commercial palaces and lovely homes!

We visited her in her hut outside of the city some months ago, to ask her if she saved Seattle in 1855, by giving information to the pioneers that the woods around it were full of lurking Indians, bent on a plot to destroy it; for there is a legend that on that shadowy December night, when Seattle was in peril, and the council of Indian warriors met and resolved to destroy the town before morning, Jim, a friendly Indian, was present at the conference as a spy. He found means to warn the pioneers of their immediate danger.

The ship of war Decatur, under Captain Gansevoort, lay in the harbor. Jim, who had acted in the Indian council, secretly, in the interest of the town, had advised the chiefs to defer the attack until early in the morning, when the officers of the Decatur would be off their guard.

Night fell on the Puget Sea. The people went into the block-house to sleep, and the men of the Decatur guarded the town, taking their stations on

Middle block-house at the Cascades.

shore. As the night deepened, a thousand hostile Indians crept up to the place and awaited the morning, when the guard should go on board the ship for breakfast, and the people should come out of the block-house and go to their houses, and "set the gun behind the door."

It was on this night, according to the legend, that "Old Angeline," as she is now called, became the messenger that saved the inhabitants from destruction.

The legend has been doubted; and when we asked the short, flat-faced old woman, as she answered our knock, if she was the daughter of the chief who saved Seattle, she simply said, "Chief," grinned, and made a bow. She was ready to accept the traditional honors of the wild legend worthy of the pen of a Cooper.

On returning from our visit to old Angeline, we asked Hon. Henry Yesler, the now rich pioneer, why the princess was not better cared for by the people of the city. He himself had been generous to her. "Why," he said, "if you were to give her fifty dollars, she would give it all away before night!" Benevolent old Angeline! She ought to live in a palace instead of a hovel! Mr. Yesler doubted the local legend, but I still wished to believe it to be true.

V.

The story of "Whitman's Ride for Oregon" has been told in verse by the writer of this volume, as follows:

WHITMAN'S RIDE FOR OREGON.

I.

"An empire to be lost or won!"
   And who four thousand miles will ride
   And climb to heaven the Great Divide,
And find the way to Washington,
   Through mountain cañons, winter snows,
   O'er streams where free the north wind blows?
Who, who will ride from Walla-Walla,
   Four thousand miles, for Oregon?

II.

"An empire to be lost or won?
   In youth to man I gave my all,
   And naught is yonder mountain wall;
If but the will of Heaven be done,
   It is not mine to live or die,
   Or count the mountains low or high,
Or count the miles from Walla-Walla.
I, I will ride for Oregon!"
   'Twas thus that Whitman made reply.

III.

"An empire to be lost or won?
    Bring me my Cayuse pony, then,
    And I will thread old ways again,
Beneath the gray skies' crystal sun.
'Twas on those altars of the air
    I raised the flag, and saw below
    The measureless Columbia flow;
The Bible oped, and bowed in prayer,
    And gave myself to God anew,
And felt my spirit newly born;
    And to my mission I'll be true,
And from the vale of Walla-Walla
    I'll ride again for Oregon.

IV.

"I'm not my own; myself I've given,
    To bear to savage hordes the Word;
If on the altars of the heaven
    I'm called to die, it is the Lord.
The herald may not wait or choose,
    'Tis his the summons to obey;
To do his best, or gain or lose,
    To seek the Guide and not the way.
He must not miss the cross, and I
    Have ceased to think of life or death;

My ark I've builded—heaven is nigh,
 And earth is but a morning's breath!
Go, then, my Cayuse pony bring;
 The hopes that seek myself are gone,
And from the vale of Walla-Walla
 I'll ride again for Oregon."

v.

He disappeared, as not his own,
 He heard the warning ice winds sigh;
The smoky sun-flames o'er him shone,
 On whitened altars of the sky,
As up the mountain-sides he rose;
 The wandering eagle round him wheeled,
The partridge fled, the gentle roes,
 And oft his Cayuse pony reeled
Upon some dizzy crag, and gazed
 Down cloudy chasms, falling storms,
While higher yet the peaks upraised
 Against the winds their giant forms.
On, on and on, past Idaho,
 On past the mighty Saline sea,
His covering at night the snow,
 His only sentinel a tree.
On, past Portneuf's basaltic heights,
 On where the San Juan Mountains lay,

Through sunless days and starless nights,
   Toward Taos and far Sante Fé.
O'er table-lands of sleet and hail,
   Through pine-roofed gorges, cañons cold,
Now fording streams incased in mail
   Of ice, like Alpine knights of old,
Still on, and on, forgetful on,
   Till far behind lay Walla-Walla,
And far the fields of Oregon.

VI.

The winter deepened, sharper grew
   The hail and sleet, the frost and snow:
Not e'en the eagle o'er him flew,
   And scarce the partridge's wing below.
The land became a long white sea,
   And then a deep with scarce a coast;
The stars refused their light, till he
   Was in the wildering mazes lost.
He droppèd rein, his stiffened hand
   Was like a statue's hand of clay!
"My trusty beast, 'tis the command;
   Go on, I leave to thee the way.
I must go on, I must go on,
   Whatever lot may fall to me,
On, 'tis for others' sake I ride—

For others I may never see,
 And dare thy clouds, O Great Divide,
  Not for myself, O Walla-Walla,
 Not for myself, O Washington,
But for thy future, Oregon."

VII.

And on and on the dumb beast pressed
 Uncertain, and without a guide,
And found the mountain's curves of rest
 And sheltered ways of the Divide.
His feet grew firm, he found the way
 With storm-beat limbs and frozen breath,
As keen his instincts to obey
 As was his master's eye of faith—
Still on and on, still on and on,
 And far and far grew Walla-Walla,
And far the fields of Oregon.

VIII.

That spring, a man with frozen feet
 Came to the marble halls of state,
And told his mission but to meet
 The chill of scorn, the scoff of hate.

"Is Oregon worth saving?" asked
    The treaty-makers from the coast;
And him the Church with questions tasked,
    And said, "Why did you leave your post?"
Was it for this that he had braved
    The warring storms of mount and sky?
Yes!—yet that empire he had saved,
    And to his post went back to die—
Went back to die for others' sake,
    Went back to die from Washington,
Went back to die for Walla-Walla,
    For Idaho and Oregon.

IX.

At fair Walla-Walla one may see
    The city of the Western North,
And near it graves unmarked there be
    That cover souls of royal worth;
The flag waves o'er them in the sky
    Beneath whose stars are cities born,
And round them mountain-castled lie
    The hundred states of Oregon.

VI.

MOUNT SAINT HELENS.

WE refer to the snowy range to the west, which terminates in the great dome that now bears that name. There was once a great lava-flood in the Northwest, and Mount Hood, Mount Adams, Mount Saint Helens, and Mount Tacoma (Rainier) are but great ash-heaps that were left by the stupendous event.

THE END.

www.ingramcontent.com/pod-product-compliance
Lightning Source LLC
Chambersburg PA
CBHW031940230426
43672CB00010B/1996